Young
People's
Science
Encyclopedia

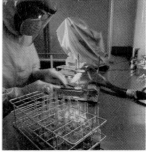

## Mo

Mosquito
Moss
Mössbauer, Rudolf
Moths
Motion
Motion pictures
Motor
Mountains
Mouse
Mouth

## Mu

Mucilage
Mucous membrane
Mucus
Mulberry
Mulch
Mule
Muller, Hermann
Muller, Paul
Mullet
Multiple birth
Multiple sclerosis
Mumps
Munitions
Murre
Muscle system
Muscle tissue
Muscular dystrophy
Mushrooms
Musical instruments
Musk
Muskrat
Mussel
Mustang
Mustard
Mutation
Mutism

## My

Myelitis
Myna
Myrtle
Myxedema

## Na

Nadir
Nail
Narcissus
Narcotics
Nasturtium
Natural bridge
Natural gas
Natural resources
Naturalist
Nature
Nausea
Nautical mile
Nautilus
Navigation

## Ne

Nearsightedness
Nebula
Nectar
Nectarine
Neele, Louis
Nemathelminthes
Nematocyst
Neodymium
Neon
Nephridia
Nephritis
Neptune
Neptunium
Nerve cell
Nervous system
Nettle

Neutralization
Neutrino
Neutron
Neutron star
Newton, Sir Isaac

## Ni

Niche
Nickel
Nicolle, Charles
Nicotine
Night-blooming
 plants
Nighthawk
Nightingale
Niobium
Nitrate
Nitration
Nitric acid
Nitrogen
Nitrogen cycle
Nitroglycerin
Nitrous acid

## No

Nobel Prize
Nobelium
Nocturnal habits
Node
Noise
Nonmetal
Normality
North America
North Atlantic drift
Nose
Notochord
Nova
Novocaine

## Nu

Nuclear energy
Nuclear particles
Nuclear reactor
Nuclear science
Nucleic acid
Nucleoprotein
Numeral systems
Nutcracker
Nuthatch
Nutmeg
Nutrition
Nuts

Nylon

## Oa

Oak
Oarfish
Oasis
Oat

Obesity
Observatory

## Oc

Ocean
Oceanography
Ochoa, Servero
Octopus

Oersted, Hans

## Oh

Ohm
Ohm, George
Ohmmeter

Oil
Oil gland

# YOUNG PEOPLE'S
# SCIENCE ENCYCLOPEDIA

Edited by the Staff of
NATIONAL COLLEGE OF EDUCATION, Evanston, Illinois

## ASSOCIATE EDITORS

# Young People's
# SCIENCE
# Encyclopedia

*Edited by the Staff of*
**NATIONAL COLLEGE OF EDUCATION**
*Evanston, Illinois*

## Volume 12/Mo-Oi

 CHILDRENS PRESS ™

CHICAGO

Photographs

Page 2:   Skylab space station (NASA)

Page 3:   *Top to Bottom:*
          Wheatfield (U.S.D.A. Photo)
          Technician capping Abbokinase (Abbott Laboratories)
          Spider (Macmillan Science Company)
          View of Earth (NASA)
          Space Shuttle (NASA)
          Bahama coral reef (Macmillan Science Company)

Cover:   Design by Sandra Gelak
         Yerkes Observatory (James P. Rowan)
         Sea Anemone (James P. Rowan)
         Big Thompson River Canyon (James P. Rowan)

Library of Congress Catalog Card Number: 67-17925

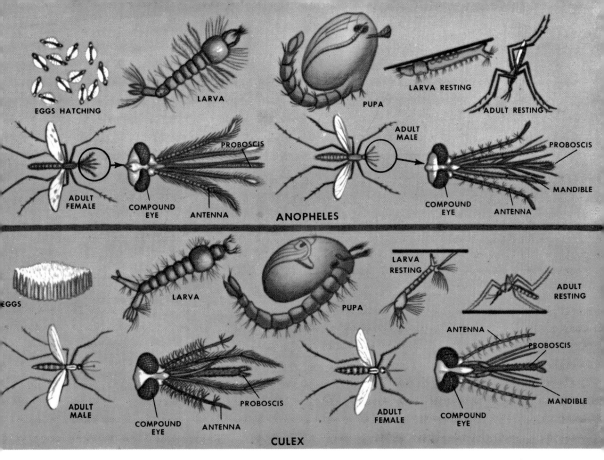

**The life history of a mosquito and the parts of its body**

**Mosquito** (muss-KEE-toh) The many kinds of INSECTS called mosquitoes are found everywhere on Earth except in freezing weather and on deserts in dry seasons. Some kinds live near swamps and lakes. Others live in drier places but can lay eggs in tiny water holes or cans—even in cracks between stems and on leaves high in trees.

Over 2,000 kinds are known, but only about 30 are pests. The worst diseases carried to man by certain mosquitoes are MALARIA, *dengue,* and YELLOW FEVER.

All mosquitoes are related to flies: they have sucking mouthparts. But only female mosquitoes' mouthparts can go into other animals' (and people's) skins. The females thus get a meal of blood. The males merely sip plant juices.

Young mosquitoes go through two stages of development. These are the LARVAE (wrigglers) and the PUPAE. Both live in water.

*Aedes aegypti* is an example of a disease carrier. The female that inserts its *proboscis* (mouthpart) into the skin of a person who has yellow fever draws into its body some of the VIRUSES of that disease. Then she may transmit the disease to another person. By contrast, the common "singing Culex" *(C. pipiens)* may be harmless or, in some cases, may carry germs of sleeping sickness or certain other diseases.

The female mosquito must have her blood meal before she matures and lays her eggs. Thereafter, she flies to water and deposits the eggs. In a few days, the eggs hatch into larvae. Later, slow-moving pupae form. Finally, the adult bursts from the pupa, ready to fly.

The insecticide DDT was once used to destroy harmful mosquitoes until it was found to accumulate in animal and, eventually, human tissues. Presently, organic phosphate compounds that are BIODEGRADABLE are used. They do not persist too long in nature and are thought not to pollute the environment. D.A.B.

SEE ALSO: INSECTA, METAMORPHOSIS

### HOW DOES A MOSS REPRODUCE ITSELF?

1. Find a glass jar with an opening large enough to get your hand inside. Make a plaster of Paris mixture and pour it into the cover of a shoe box. Just as it begins to harden, push the side of the jar slightly into the surface of the mixture. The plaster will serve as a base to hold your glass terrarium.

2. Take a hike into the woods to gather moss. It will usually be found in shady, moist places. Transfer plants and plenty of rich soil into the jar. Water well and do not keep your moss house in direct sunlight.

3. Examine the tops of the little upright shoots with a hand lens. One small head will produce the sperms and another will form the eggs. After the egg is fertilized a little stalk grows up out of the female head. At the top of the stalk is the capsule containing the spores. When the capsule breaks open the spores fall to the soil and germinate into new plants. A little sulfur sprinkled in the soil will prevent growth of mold.

**Moss** These small green plants form velvety cushions in a wide range of places. There are 14,000 kinds of mosses. They live from the warm tropics up to the cold Arctic regions. Most mosses are land plants. A few species are found in streams.

Moss has no true roots, stems, LEAVES, FLOWERS, or FRUITS. They lack the conducting tubes or canals of higher plants. This factor limits their size since much of the material and food must be passed from one cell to another. Having CHLOROPHYLL, they are independent and can produce their own food.

All mosses reproduce by ALTERNATION OF GENERATIONS. The *gametophyte* generation is the most conspicuous. It has a bushy appearance. The erect stalk or *thallus* is not a true stem yet looks like one. It bears leaf-like scales. These are only one cell thick except along the midrib which is composed of several layers of cells. The stalk is anchored to the ground or substrate by rootlike structures called *rhizoids*. The male and female plants may be on the same plant or on separate plants. The *archegonium* is the female stalk which produces the egg. The *antheridi-um* or male structure produces hundreds of sperms. A biflagellate sperm needs water to reach the egg. Fertilization may occur during a rain or heavy dew.

The *sporophyte* generation begins to develop from the zygote or fertilized egg. It is composed of a foot which is anchored in the female gametophyte. From this a stalk or *seta* develops. The capsule or *sporangium* is on top of the seta. The sporophyte plant has some chlorophyll but is almost entirely dependent upon the gametophyte for its food supply. In the capsule, spore mother cells are diploid. After MEIOSIS they produce microscopic haploid spores. When the capsule dries up, these spores are released and dispersed by wind. A spore which lands in a moist shady place will begin to germinate. It grows into a hypha-like green structure called a *protonema*. This is the beginning of another gametophyte generation.

Mosses belong to class Musci, the largest and most complex group of plants in the phylum Bryophyta. There are three subclasses. The subclass Sphagnobrya has one genus, *Sphagnum*, which includes about 300 species. They are commonly called *bog* or *peat* mosses, for they inhabit acid swamps and bogs. When these plants are added to garden soil, its water-holding power is generally increased. Peat moss is also used in packing other plants for shipping.

The subclass Andreaeobrya has two genera and are commonly called *granite* mosses.

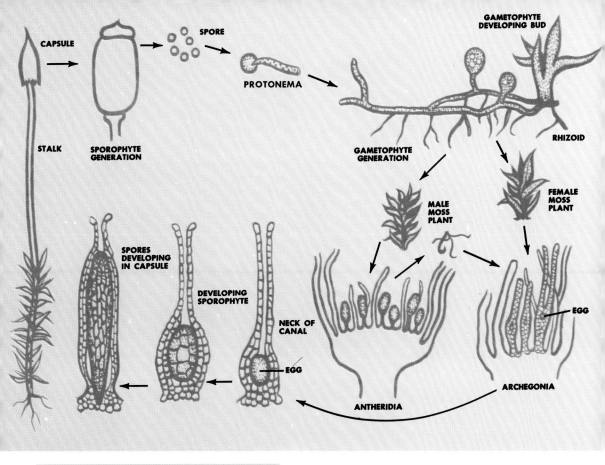

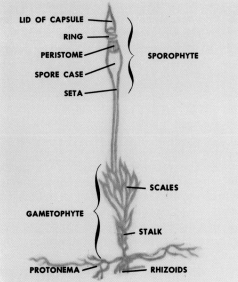

**Parts of a moss plant, showing the gametophyte and sporophyte generations**

widely distributed kinds in the world. The majority, however, inhabit the temperate regions. They are usually found on acid soil in shady places. They break up rocks and improve fertility of the soil.     H. J. C.

SEE ALSO: BRYOPHYTES; PLANTS, CLASSIFICATION OF; SPORE FORMATION

## Mössbauer, Rudolf (1929- )

Mössbauer, a German, was a co-winner of the 1961 NOBEL PRIZE in physics. He is known for the discovery of the *Mössbauer effect.*

Mössbauer studied the emission and absorption of gamma rays from atomic nuclei tightly bound in a crystal. This produced a "recoil-free" environment. The gamma rays showed a wavelength and frequency more constant than ever before noted. A highly charged atomic nucleus will ordinarily recoil like a gun being fired. Energy of the emissions is altered or decreased much like the loss of energy of a bullet due to the recoil process. Mössbauer experiments produced a highly accurate tool called the Mössbauer effect. It is useful in nuclear, chemical, and solid-state physics.
                                                                                                    A.J.H.

They thrive in Alpine regions and on barren rocks in the frigid Arctic areas. Economically they are of little use to man. Some species in the far north are eaten by wildlife since it is the only vegetation available to them.

The subclass Eubrya includes eighty families of the true mosses. They are the most

(1) Sphinx moth that lays eggs on tomato plants and makes cocoons in the ground; (2) the io moth, with eye-like wing spots; (3) Promethea moth; (4) luna moth with spurred wings; and (5) silkworm moths

Courtesy Society For Visual Education, Inc

**Moths** These are insects with scaly wings. Like BUTTERFLIES, moths belong in the order Lepidoptera, meaning "scaly winged." Moths have feathery feelers or antennae while butterflies have knobs on the ends of theirs. At rest, butterflies hold their wings up while moths either hold their wings out flat or fold them. Moths are *nocturnal*, coming out at night. Butterflies are *diurnal*, coming out during the daytime. There are thousands of kinds of moths.

Some moths, like the *sphinx* moth, pollinate plants, while many serve as food for fish, amphibians, and birds. Some, like the *clothes* moth, have LARVAE or CATERPILLARS that eat clothing. Other moth larvae damage crops and some make GALLS on leaves and stems or make tunnels through them.

Moths have complete METAMORPHOSIS. An egg develops into a caterpillar that molts several times. Each molt represents a stage in the life cycle. The form of an insect after a molt is called an *instar*. Due to growth between molts, each instar is larger than the one before. The final instar pupates by spinning a COCOON. After a resting period, often over the winter, the adult moth emerges.

Aside from size, larval instars do not show much change in structure. Caterpillars feed while the pupae do not. The pupal stage, while called quiet or quiescent, is actually an active one since a complete change of struc-

ture takes place. Larval tissues are destroyed and adult tissues are formed from centers called *imaginal disks*. These changes, and those taking place in the egg and in the caterpillars, are all inherited. It is possible that different sets of GENES act at different times during the life cycle. The "switching on and off" of different sets is controlled by hormones secreted by *neurohemal organs*. These organs may be stimulated to secrete by such conditions as changes in light, temperature, and food.

In the *cecropia* moth, temperature changes activate the secretion of a brain hormone, BH. Neurosecretory cells in the brain send AXONS to glands called *corpora cardiaca*. These are located behind the brain and near the *dorsal aorta*. The BH is discharged by the axons into these glands where it is stored and released into the blood. The BH stimulates another gland (prothoracic) to produce the molting hormone *ecdysone* which acts on body tissues to cause them to begin to form adult tissues. Other glands, the *corpora allata*, secrete a juvenile hormone, JH, which inhibits development of adult structure but allows growth and molting to take place. Thus, larval stages are formed when the concentration of JH is high. With each instar the concentration of JH drops. In the last, it is too low to prevent development of adult structure. At this time, pupation occurs and the caterpillar begins to change into an adult.

J. C. K.

SEE ALSO: BUTTERFLIES, CATERPILLAR, COCOON, INSECTICIDES, METAMORPHOSIS, PLANT PESTS

# Motion

**Motion** Motion refers to the movement of an object from one place to another along some particular path. There are usually a number of paths and a number of different types of motion a moving body can exhibit. The motion itself may be divided into two types, *linear* and *circular*. Linear motion refers only to that part of the path where an object moves in a straight line. Circular motion applies to that part of the path which is curved. The concepts of circular motion are more difficult than those of linear motion and are beyond the scope of this book.

The motion of an object can be studied by observing it for a period of time. The distance traveled by the object may be the same for each equal interval of time. If so, the movement is referred to as *uniform motion*. In cases of uniform linear motion, a body will move along at a constant speed and with zero acceleration.

The speed of a body having uniform linear motion is defined as the distance the body travels divided by the time required by the body to travel this distance. The equation is:

$$s = d/t$$

where $s$ is the speed, $d$ is the distance traveled, and $t$ the time required. Since $d$ can be expressed in any unit of length, such as feet or centimeters, and time is expressed in seconds or hours, the units of speed would then be feet per second in the British system of units, or centimeters per second in the metric system. Of course, miles per hour and kilometers per hour are also used.

It is necessary to distinguish here between *speed* and *velocity*. Although both speed and velocity are expressed in the same units,

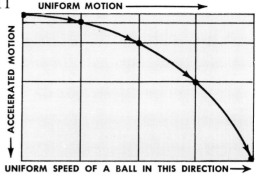

UNIFORM SPEED OF A BALL IN THIS DIRECTION →
AND ACCELERATED MOTION DOWNWARD, DUE TO
GRAVITY PRODUCE THIS TYPE OF MOTION GRAPH

A ball thrown forward at uniform speed is also acted upon by the downward acceleration of gravity. Its path can be shown by this type of motion graph

they are not the same quantity. Speed refers only to the distance the body travels per unit of time. VELOCITY not only refers to the speed at which the body travels but also includes the direction in which the body is moving—and is called a *vector*. A vector is a quantity with direction and magnitude.

To illustrate the difference between speed and velocity, consider the case of an automobile turning a corner at a constant speed. The speed of the automobile is considered constant because it moves the same distance during each unit of time, but the *direction* of motion changes, hence *velocity* changes.

Motion which is both uniform and linear is quite easy to imagine and study. Unfortunately, this type of motion is not the most common. Many bodies travel in a manner which does not exhibit the properties of uniform motion. For instance, it is known that when a body falls toward the earth, it does so with its speed becoming faster and faster as it approaches the earth. When riding in an automobile, the driver may "speed up" to pass another automobile and then return to his original speed. The period during which the car is speeding up and slowing down again is a period of non-uniform mo-

Linear motion of these objects is: (A) uniform in distance and time, (B) accelerated or speeded-up, (C) decelerated or slowed-down

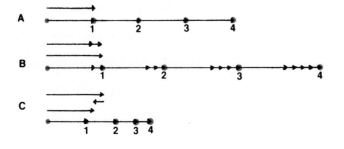

tion. Cases where nonuniform motion is preceded and followed by uniform motion are quite common.

Consider this example. If the car acquired an additional velocity of 4 feet (122 centimeters) per second in the first second and another 4 feet (122 centimeters) per second in the next second, it is said to have a *pickup* or ACCELERATION of 4 feet (122 centimeters) per second in each second. By the end of four seconds it will have increased its velocity by 16 feet (488 centimeters) per second. This type of motion is called *uniformly accelerated motion*.

The average acceleration of a body is defined as the change of its velocity during any interval of time divided by that interval of time. The definition is based on *change* of velocity rather than total distance traveled. In equation form, acceleration may be written as:

$$a = \frac{v_f - v_c}{t}$$

where $v_o$ is the velocity of the object at the beginning of the time interval and $v_f$ is the velocity of the object at the end of the interval, $t$ is the duration of the interval and $a$ is the acceleration. Units of acceleration are normally expressed as feet per second per second or centimeters per second per second.

There is a great deal to be said about objects or bodies which exhibit motion that is a combination of uniform linear motion and uniform accelerated motion. Consider a baseball thrown in a horizontal direction. Neglecting the resistance offered by the air, there is nothing to increase the speed of the ball nor is there anything to slow the speed while it is in the air. Thus, the horizontal motion of the ball is uniform. At the same time that the ball is traveling toward the batter, it is being acted upon by gravity just as any other object which is free to fall. The falling or vertical motion is accelerated by the force of gravity so that the motion in the vertical direction is uniformly accelerated motion. The horizontal motion has no effect on the vertical motion, nor does the vertical motion have any effect on the horizontal. The fact that these motions act independently of one another allows each one to be studied separately.          A. E. L.

SEE ALSO: FALLING BODIES, PENDULUM

**Motion, perpetual**  see Perpetual motion machine

**Motion pictures**  Motion pictures are made by a camera which takes many still pictures very rapidly, one after another. These pictures are shown by a PROJECTOR which flashes them on a screen so fast that they seem to blend into one continuous moving picture.

These "stills" seem to be one continuous picture because the viewer's eyes play a trick called PERSISTENCE OF VISION. When the eyes see an image, they hold onto it in the form of a visual memory for a fraction of a second after it is gone. A person sees something when it is no longer there. The separate still pictures which make up a motion picture flash on and off the screen so fast that the images do not have time to die out between pictures. Each picture shows a slightly more advanced step of some act of motion. The image of the first picture stays in the eyes until the second picture is seen and so on, causing each picture to blend into the next.

**A small motion picture camera for home use**

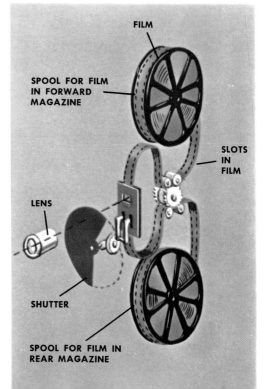

FILM

SPOOL FOR FILM IN FORWARD MAGAZINE

SLOTS IN FILM

LENS

SHUTTER

SPOOL FOR FILM IN REAR MAGAZINE

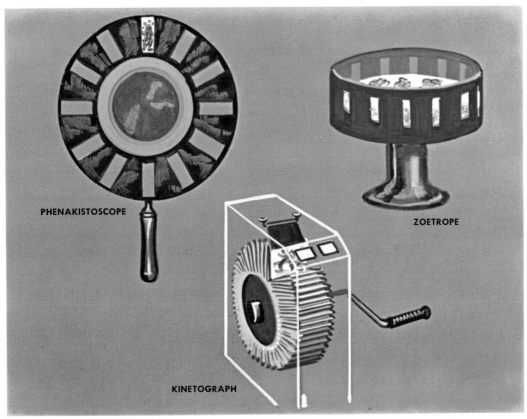

PHENAKISTOSCOPE

ZOETROPE

KINETOGRAPH

**These three devices were early attempts at giving the illusion of motion to pictures**

A motion picture is made by passing a strip of film through the camera behind the lens. The film is advanced in small intervals (frames). Each time the film stops the shutter opens and a picture is taken. There are usually 18 frames per second taken in silent film and 24 frames per second for sound films. The usual sizes for motion picture film are 8 millimeter (mm.) for home movies; 16 mm. for professional filming; and 35 mm. for theatrical filming.

When the film is run through a projector, each picture is pulled into position in front of a strong light and left there briefly. The shutter opens when the picture is in position, and the light throws a shadow of the picture on the screen; then the shutter closes while another picture is pulled into position. This happens at the same speed at which the pictures were taken. Persistence of vision causes each still picture to blend into the next, giving the effect of motion.

It is possible to record SOUND on the film at the same time the picture is taken. The sound waves are changed to an electric current which passes through a sensitive light bulb, causing a pattern of light and dark areas—the *sound track*—to be photographed on one side of the film. This process is reversed in the projector, using a *photoelectric* cell connected to a loudspeaker.

Animated pictures of one kind or another are very old. The ancient Egyptians knew that viewing a series of pictures in quick succession would give an illusion of movement. In 1824, Dr. Peter Roget, an Englishman, first suggested that the use of the principle of persistence of vision might result in a moving picture. This led to the development, in the 1830's, of the *phenakistoscope* and the *zoetrope*. In both machines a series of pictures of an object in motion could be viewed through slits in a rotating disk.

Muybridge, in the 1870's, was the first to photograph motion successfully when he used many separate cameras to take pictures of a running horse. However, the photography of motion with a single camera had to wait until 1888, when Eastman perfected photographic roll film. Shortly after this, Edison produced his *kinetograph,* a machine which took a series of pictures on a roll

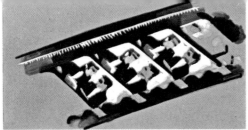

The sound track moves past a photoelectric cell which transforms light pulses into electric pulses, later changed into sound

film, and the *kinetoscope,* a machine for viewing them. The viewer looked into the kinetoscope as he turned a large wheel on which hundreds of photographs flipped by, each lighted for a second.

There was still no way for large audiences to see a motion picture together. C. Francis Jenkin's *phantascope* (1894) and Thomas Armat's *vitascope* (1895) were the first projectors made. Both machines moved a long film of thousands of photographs past a projecting lens in much the same way as is done today. Many improvements have since been made in cameras, film, and projectors. Sound was added to motion pictures in the 1920's and color by the 1930's.

*Cinerama* and *Cinemascope* are trade names of two recent developments in motion pictures. They both give a three-dimensional effect because the viewer sees what is going on not only directly in front of him but also out of the corners of his eyes.

Cinerama requires three projectors which show the picture in sections. The center projector shows what a standard machine shows, and the other two show what an observer would see if he turned his head right or left.

Cinemascope, Vistavision, and the other wide-angle lens processes use a single projector. *Vistavision* uses standard 35 mm. film but a double frame-size picture. *Todd-AO* and the other special processes use 56 mm. film. An *anamorphoscopic* lens unit is put on a standard 35 mm. camera. It takes in a scene which is the same height but three times as wide as that which a conventional lens records and squeezes it onto a standard-width 35 mm. film. The compressed image on the film looks thin and distorted, like an image on a funhouse mirror. Another anamorphoscopic lens on the projector expands the picture to natural proportions. A screen three times standard width is used. It is curved so that the distance from the projector is the same to all parts of the screen. This keeps the picture in sharp focus throughout its width.          E. R. B.
SEE ALSO: EDISON, THOMAS A.; FILM; PHOTO-ELECTRICITY; PHOTOGRAPHY

**Motor** A motor is a type of machine which provides motion. The words *motor* and *engine* are frequently interchanged. Today, motors are widely used in automobiles, boats, trains, and electrical appliances.

The most common type in use today is the *electric motor.* In a modern house the refrigerator, vacuum cleaner, furnace, food mixer, electric train, power drill, and many other appliances all use electric motors.

Electric motors are extremely practical because the electric current to operate them can be conducted through wires. These wires provide a convenient means of transporting electrical ENERGY from an available source to where it is needed. An electric motor changes electrical energy into mechanical energy. This change in energy is made by *magnetism.*

In the home the simplest electric motor is the *electric bell.* The bell is rung by a back and forth motion caused by the turning on and off of ELECTROMAGNETS. Early electric motors worked in the same manner.

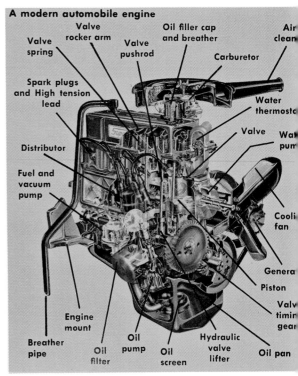

A modern automobile engine

Valve rocker arm — Valve spring — Valve pushrod — Oil filler cap and breather — Air cleaner — Carburetor — Spark plugs and High tension lead — Water thermostat — Valve — Water pump — Distributor — Fuel and vacuum pump — Cooling fan — Generator — Piston — Valve timing gear — Engine mount — Breather pipe — Oil filter — Oil pump — Oil screen — Hydraulic valve lifter — Oil pan

### HOW DOES A MOTOR WORK?

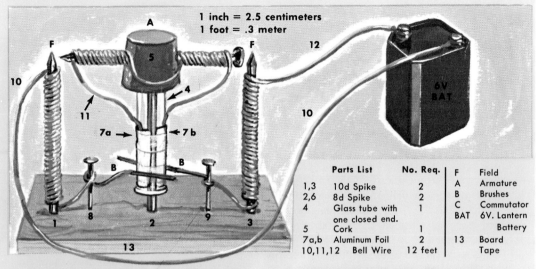

1 inch = 2.5 centimeters
1 foot = .3 meter

| | Parts List | No. Req. | | |
|---|---|---|---|---|
| | | | F | Field |
| 1,3 | 10d Spike | 2 | A | Armature |
| 2,6 | 8d Spike | 2 | B | Brushes |
| 4 | Glass tube with | 1 | C | Commutator |
| | one closed end. | | BAT | 6V. Lantern |
| 5 | Cork | 1 | | Battery |
| 7a,b | Aluminum Foil | 2 | 13 | Board |
| 10,11,12 | Bell Wire | 12 feet | | Tape |

1. Read the directions first. Have all the materials. Follow the diagram carefully. All wires must be wound on the nails in the same direction. (Study ends of nails in diagram.) Drive spikes (1,2,3) as shown. Insert spike (6) through cork near one end. Make a hole in center of the other end of the cork for a tight fit on the glass tube (4). Insert tube. Spike (6) must be very close to spikes (1,3). The glass tube must turn freely on spike (2). Cut two strips of foil (7a, 7b) and tape them to the glass tube leaving a little space between them on both sides. Drive two small nails (8,9) into the board about one inch from spike (2) and on either side of it.

2. Wind 100 turns of wire on each spike (1,3) leaving two inches of wire at the bottom and ten inches free at the top. Remove insulation for one inch at each end of the wires. Wind each lower wire once around the small nail (8,9) nearest it.

3. Wind 40 turns of wire around each end of spike (6) leaving enough wire at the ends of the spike to reach under the foil. Remove the insulation and tape them securely under the foil, as shown. Place the glass tube over spike (2). Adjust the wires (brushes) on nails (8,9) so each contacts the foil (commutator) under slight pressure on opposite sides of the tube.

4. Connect each ten-inch length of wire coming from the upper end of spikes (1,3) to the terminals of a six-volt lantern battery. Give the armature a push to start it. If it does not run, check the contacts at the brushes (B) and commutator (C) to insure that electrical continuity is maintained except when the space between the foil pieces passes by. When the space is under the brushes, the spike (6) should point to spikes (1,3).

A *rotary* motor is unlike the electric motor in a bell, which uses only the force of attraction from magnets fixed in one position and is turned on and off periodically. The rotary motor utilizes the combined forces of both attraction and repulsion. Much like a generator (DYNAMO), the rotary motor has two kinds of magnets—field magnets and an ARMATURE. The field magnets may be either permanent or electromagnets, and both are stationary. The armature, an electromagnet, rotates as the direction of the current supplied to it is periodically reversed. The COMMUTATOR reverses the flow of current to the armature at the correct moment to keep the armature rotating.

Electric motors vary in size from small electric clock motors to sizes which develop 40,000 HORSEPOWER or more. These large motors are used to propel ocean ships.

The diesel-electric train has a diesel in-

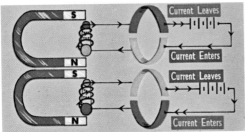

Courtesy Society For Visual Education, Inc.

**When the electric current flows into the different halves of the commutator, the current in the armature changes direction**

Macmillan Science Company

ternal combustion motor which generates electricity. The electricity is then carried to electric motors, which propel the train.

Automobiles, motor boats, trucks, and buses burn gasoline in their internal combustion engines.

Jet, rocket, and atomic motors will be very important in future transportation. Atomic motors propel ships and submarines. Rocket motors develop more power than any other motor yet engineered. P. F. D.
SEE ALSO: AUTOMOBILE, ELECTRICITY, ENGINE, MAGNET, ROCKET ENGINES

**Mount Everest** see Asia

**Mount Rainier** see North America

**Mountain goat** see Goat

**Mountain laurel** see Laurel, Rhododendron

**Mountain lion** see Cat family

**Mountains** Mountains are the highest areas on earth. In total area, they compose a much smaller percentage of the earth's total land surface than do PLAINS. Compared with hills, they are more massive and rugged. To be a mountain, a land form, from its lowest to its highest point, must be taller than 2,000 feet (610 meters). This means that many of the hills often called mountains are not mountains at all.

**A view of the Alps Mountains of Switzerland from the peak Mount Blanc**

Buchsbaum

Many of the most awe-inspiring and interesting features of the earth's surface are exhibited within some of the great masses of mountains on various continents. High glaciated mountains are sharp and bold because of the long continued ice scour. Almost vertical walls of solid rock may rise abruptly. In a single glaciated valley may be several small lakes.

There are several basic processes by which mountains are formed:

1. The *uplifting* of huge masses of igneous rocks, especially granite, gives rise to many mountains.

2. Volcanic cones are formed by the *eruption* of huge quantities of ash, LAVA, and other materials.

3. Some block mountains are formed by *faulting*. This is the uplifting of a block of rock, which usually has on one side a steep face called a *fault scarp,* and on the other a more gentle sloping surface.

4. *Folding* may cause rock strata to be bent upward.

There are also several classes of mountains:

1. *Peaks* are considered the highest points in a mountain mass.

2. A *range* is usually a continuous arrangement of peaks, ridges, and valleys.

3. A *cordillera* is a large regional group of mountain systems.

4. A *volcanic* cone is a form of mountain peak that is in some cases isolated from a system or range.

5. A *system* is a group of mountain ranges. Mountains sometimes serve as

## Mourning dove

natural boundaries between countries. They often contain rich mineral deposits useful to our economy. They are eroded by streams, winds, and glaciers. One can also observe on some of the high mountains both the timberline and the snowline.

Most geologists now believe that the formation of great mountain chains is directly related to the theory of CONTINENTAL DRIFT: mountains occur when continents collide and great compressional forces cause large sections of the earth's crust to buckle. The Himalaya Mountains of India are good examples of this type of mountain building.

V.V.N./P.P.S.

SEE ALSO: EARTH, GEOLOGY

**Mourning dove** see Dove

**Mouse** Mice are gnawing animals. The difference between mice and rats is mostly one of size. The rat and mouse family is the largest of the MAMMAL group. The small *house* mouse has soft, brownish fur, a pointed nose, large ears, and a long, hairless tail.

Gnawing animals are called *rodents*. Their teeth grow continuously because gnawing wears them down. Small wild mice are often called *voles,* heavier tailless ones *lemmings,* and larger ones rats.

Mice have NOCTURNAL HABITS and live in burrows or in tunnels made through grass roots. House mice build nests of odds and ends of household materials. These are usually put in some out-of-the-way place.

In the southern United States, *harvest* mice are the common ones in the fields. They are about half the size of the house mice. Farther north, the *white-footed deer* mice are common. These are also called *wood* mice. Also present are the common *meadow* mice or *field* voles. Any of these may enter homes during colder weather. *Jumping* or *kangaroo* mice are not true mice. They belong to another family. These have long tails and hind legs like kangaroos, but they do not have abdominal pouches since they are rodents rather than MARSUPIALS. J. C. K.

SEE ALSO: RODENTIA, WHITE MICE

The common house mouse is one of the world's most destructive pests

A few of the many different kinds of mice: (top left) grasshopper mouse, (top right) white-footed mouse, (bottom left) lemming in winter, and (bottom right) jumping mouse

**Mouth** The mouth is the opening in the head of an animal which leads to the digestive tract. In higher animals, it has two parts: the space between teeth and lips, and a cavity equipped to hold and chew food.

In lower animals, the mouth is simpler. Lampreys have funnel-shaped mouths used for sucking, and no jaw. Amphibians have no palates. Palates first appear in reptiles.

J. C. K.

**Mucilage** (MEW-sih-lij) Mucilage is a kind of liquid gum used to stick things together. It comes from plants such as SEAWEED and from the coverings of seeds. The backs of postage stamps are coated with mucilage.

SEE: ADHESIVES

**Mucous membrane** The mucous membrane is made of epithelial cells which secrete mucus. It lines the nose, throat and respiratory tract which have openings to the outside air.

SEE: EPITHELIAL TISSUE

**Mucus** Mucus is the thick, slippery secretion of the mucous membranes which moistens and lubricates internal body surfaces. Fish and amphibians produce mucus at the body surface.

**Mud hen** see Coot

**Mud puppy** see Salamander

Two common mulberries, the red and the white

**Mulberry** LEAVES on this tree are simple, alternate, and saw-toothed. Bark is yellow-brown. FLOWERS grow in clusters. Multiple FRUIT develops.

Paper mulberry, 50 feet (15.2 meters) tall, has red fruit. Red mulberry, 40 feet (12.2 meters) tall, has reddish-black fruit. White mulberry has white fruit. Its leaves are used to feed silkworms. These trees belong to the family Moraceae.          H.J.C.

**Mulch** Mulch is a loose layer of material such as grass clippings or straw which is kept on the surface of the ground around plants to retard weeds, prevent freezing, stop EROSION, and prevent loss of water from the soil.
SEE: SOIL TYPES

**Mule** The mule is a hybrid, a combination animal. It is the offspring of a male donkey (*jack*) and a female horse (*mare*). It is about the size of a horse but both of its ends, the ears and tail, are more like the jackass.

Mules are sterile, which means they cannot have baby mules. The reproductive organs never mature. Mules do not need a fancy diet as many horses do.

Most of the mules in the United States are used for various jobs on small farms. Their skillful footwork enables them to travel over trails too hazardous for the ordinary horse. The expression, "stubborn as a mule," is true, for they are obstinate creatures that cannot be forced to overwork. But they will work under difficult conditions and in very hot weather.          H. J. C.

**Mule deer** see Deer family

**Mullein** see Wild flowers

**Muller, Hermann J.** (1890-1967) Muller is a U.S. geneticist who was awarded the 1946 NOBEL PRIZE in physiology and medicine. He discovered that genetic *mutations* resulted from exposure to *radiation.*

Muller first experimented with the effect X ray radiation had on fruit fly eggs. The results were dramatic. The eggs exposed to radiation later produced mutants that had changes in their eyes and wing shapes, and in their entire physical appearance. Based on his findings, Muller was one of the first scientists to alert the world to the possible hazards of excessive medical use of radiation, and to the danger of nuclear fallout from atomic explosions.          P.P.S.

**Müller, Paul Heeman** (1899-1965) The 1948 NOBEL PRIZE in medicine was awarded to the Swiss chemist Paul Müller for his work with the insecticide, DDT.

Müller, a research chemist, was the first scientist to explore and prove the effectiveness of DDT as an insecticide. His discovery, DDT, was used during World War II to control the malaria mosquito. Because of its undesirable effects upon the environment, DDT is no longer used in the United States.          A.J.H.

**Mullet** The mullet is a tasty FISH found in fresh and salt, temperate and tropical shore waters. There are two families of mullet—the *gray* mullet, which has a small mouth and shiny scales, and the *red* mullet, which has bright-red or golden scales.

Striped mullet, the most common gray mullet

Multiple births are common among dogs, but occur less frequently among humans.

Argonne National Laboratories

**Multicellular organisms** see Animals, classification of; Evolution; Plants, classification of

**Multiple birth** When a mammal gives birth to more than one offspring at a time, it is called a multiple birth. Larger animals usually have a single birth, as with elephants, camels, giraffes, horses, cattle and man. In small animals, it is common to have more than one in a litter. Pigs, dogs, cats and mice can have from two to eighteen at one time. The most famous quintuplets are the Dionne sisters of Canada, born in 1934. They were the first quintuplets to have reached adult age. Since then others have survived.

There are two types of twins in man. *Fraternal* twins come from two eggs fertilized by two different sperm cells. *Identical* twins develop from an egg fertilized by a single sperm. The egg divides and separates into two cells. Each cell contains identical GENES.

HORMONES have been developed which induce OVULATION. When given these hormones by a doctor, some women have delivered as many as 9 babies at one time. To date, keeping alive all tiny babies in a nonuplet birth has not been accomplished.
B.M.H.

SEE ALSO: EMBRYOLOGY, HEREDITY

**Multiple fruits** see Fruit

**Multiple sclerosis** (skluh-ROH-siss) Multiple sclerosis is a disease of the brain and spinal cord. Healthy nerve fibers in the white matter of the NERVOUS SYSTEM in many parts of the body lose their ability to conduct impulses and deteriorate. Tough, hardened scar tissue replaces the nerve tissue.

Symptoms include paralysis, blindness, and speech difficulties. The disease is not contagious, but it may result from an early childhood viral infection.
E.S.S.
SEE ALSO: BRAIN, SPINAL CORD

**Multiple star** see Stars

**Mumps** Mumps is a contagious disease that causes the SALIVARY GLANDS to swell. Sometimes the glands under the lower jaw are affected. This is caused by a VIRUS. Swallowing is painful.

Mumps may affect the BRAIN and PANCREAS. A vaccine may prevent infection for life. Thus, it is possible that mumps may be eradicated along with measles and poliomyelitis.
B.M.H.

**Munitions** Munitions are the equipment and materials necessary to wage war. The term includes guns, ammunition, PROJECTILES, vehicles, machinery, and military stores of all kinds.
SEE: WEAPONS

**Murre** The murre is a diving bird of the AUK family. It lives in large colonies on the rocky coasts of the North Atlantic and North Pacific. It has short wings and a brownish-black body with white underside. In the far north, people eat both the bird and its large, blotched, white or bluish egg.

The murre is a member of the auk family.

**Muscle system** Worms wiggle and crawl. Grasshoppers jump. Fish can swim. Most birds can fly. Deer run. Many animals move because they have special muscle cells. These cells work together to form a tissue. These tissues form a system of muscles.

The first muscle cells to appear in the simple animals are called *myocytes*. The little HYDRA is not too active because these cells are not organized into an efficient tissue. As animals become more complex their muscles and ability to move keep pace with the other structures. The muscles in flat and round worms help them to orient their bodies. Since many of them are parasitic (live on other animals) they do not need to move far. True worms have muscles going around their bodies as well as lengthwise. This enables them to constrict and extend. Echinoderms (STARFISH, urchins, etc.) have many muscles in the tube feet of their water vascular systems.

The arthropods (insects, spiders, and crustaceans) have jointed appendages. The muscles attached to these can produce frequent, rapid movements. A housefly can move its wings 300 times per second but the tiny midge breaks the record at 1000 movements per second. The muscles of a DRAGONFLY propel it 30 miles (48 kilometers) or more per hour. The monarch BUTTERFLY has the strength to fly 1000 miles (1,609 kilometers) during its migration.

The vertebrates (animals with back-bones) have well-developed muscular systems especially adapted for survival. BIRDS have powerful breast (*pectoral*) muscles to help them fly. Reptiles have strong tail and jaw muscles to defend themselves. Many mammals have muscles adapted for running, leaping, and swimming. Without muscles food could not be eaten, the heart would not beat, nor the diaphragm move to help respiration. Movement of any kind involves cells that contract and relax.

## STRUCTURE

Man has over 600 muscles in his body. Muscles are made of bundles of long cells. Muscles may be flat and sheet-like as the ones across the back and abdomen. They may be long and spindle-shaped as the one in the upper arm that is tightened when one wants to show "how strong he is." Most muscles come in pairs. The muscles on the front of the leg are used to kick a football while the ones on the back of the leg are needed to bring the leg back into position. One set of muscles helps a person lean over, the opposite muscles take the body back to where it started.

Muscle cells can contract, or shorten, and relax, returning to their original length. This only occurs when the cells are stimulated. Nerve impulses from the brain or spinal cord,

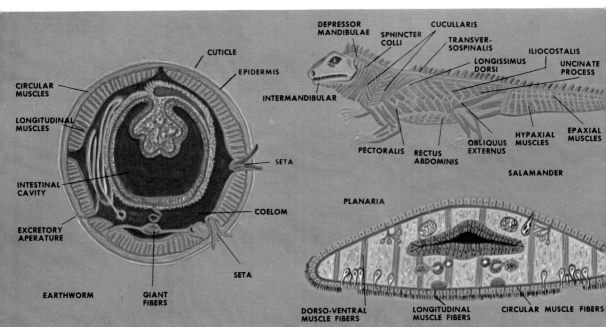

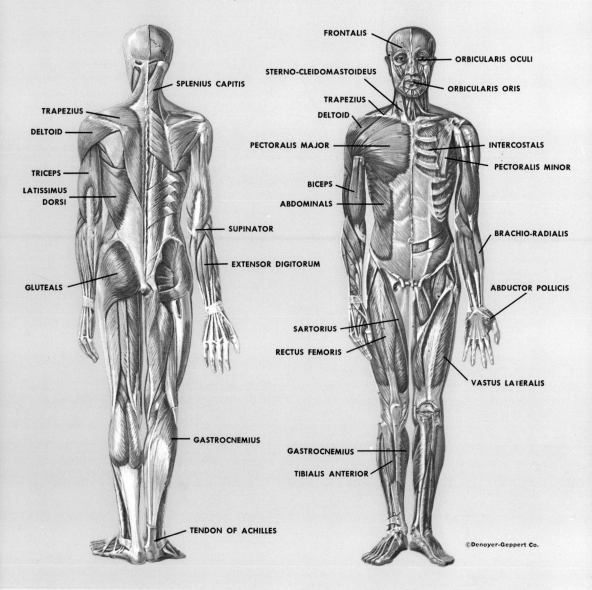

FRONTALIS
ORBICULARIS OCULI
STERNO-CLEIDOMASTOIDEUS
ORBICULARIS ORIS
TRAPEZIUS
DELTOID
PECTORALIS MAJOR
INTERCOSTALS
PECTORALIS MINOR
BICEPS
ABDOMINALS
BRACHIO-RADIALIS
ABDUCTOR POLLICIS
SARTORIUS
RECTUS FEMORIS
VASTUS LATERALIS
GASTROCNEMIUS
TIBIALIS ANTERIOR

SPLENIUS CAPITIS
TRAPEZIUS
DELTOID
TRICEPS
LATISSIMUS DORSI
SUPINATOR
EXTENSOR DIGITORUM
GLUTEALS
GASTROCNEMIUS
TENDON OF ACHILLES

©Denoyer-Geppert Co.

or from the nerve network in lower animals, reach the individual cells and cause them to contract.

Contraction of cells requires energy, so muscles must be supplied glucose (an energy source) and oxygen by the blood. They also store sugar in the form of glycogen. Much muscle energy is lost as heat, as when one becomes warm during strenuous exercise.

Muscle tissue is composed of three proteins, *myosin, myogen,* and *myoglobin.* The most abundant is myosin which combines with *actin* to form *actomyosin.* The muscle fiber consists of fibrils or long bundles of these protein molecules. These are the real contractile parts of muscles.

### FUNCTION

Muscles move the body in different directions. They are anchored at each end by bones or other structures that are moved. Some bend the arms and legs (*flexors*) while others straighten them (*extensors*). Muscles with opposite effects are called *antagonists.* Muscles that move the arm up are called *elevators,* the opposite muscles are *depressors.* *Adductors* bring arms or legs closer together, *abductors* take them away. *Pronators* turn the palm and sole down and *supinators* turn them up.

Muscle cells function according to the *all-or-none* law. Each cell contracts to its utmost or not at all. Some people are stronger than others because more individual cells are stimulated to contract at one time. Exercise increases the diameter of each fiber. This further increases strength, endurance, and efficiency.

How well muscles function (mechanical efficiency) depends upon several factors.

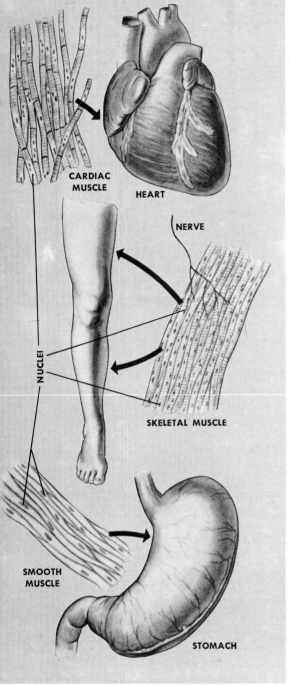

CARDIAC MUSCLE

HEART

NERVE

NUCLEI

SKELETAL MUSCLE

SMOOTH MUSCLE

STOMACH

TODAY'S HEALTH published by AMERICAN MEDICAL ASSOCIATION

**Muscle tissue has become highly-developed and specialized to meet special body needs**

The *rhythm* of movement is important. Fast, jerky actions are less effective than coordinated movements. Mechanical efficiency in over-weight people is less than in those with a proper height-weight balance. Age plays a significant role in muscular activity. Usually a man of 20 is more active and efficient than a man of 50. A person who trains in a muscular activity is obviously in better condition than one who does not. Most strenuous activity requires a "warming up" period.

*Fatigue* occurs when muscles fail to react to the stimulus and therefore will not contract. Fatigue may be caused by one or more of these conditions: overexertion, poor circulation, lack of food and oxygen, or disease. It sets in as waste, chiefly lactic acid, accumulated in the muscles. Lactic acid is sent to the liver where it is converted into sugar or glycogen if it is going to be stored. When this occurs a person gets his "second wind."

The muscles in the body are never completely relaxed. This slight contraction is termed *muscle tonus*. It is a reflex. Muscles also resist being stretched to their fullest. A person with good posture has good muscle tone. Poor posture encourages fatigue. One's appearance and comfort is very dependent upon the muscular system. H. J. C.
SEE ALSO: ARTHROPODA, MUSCLE TISSUE, NERVOUS SYSTEM

**Muscle tissue** The heart beats. The stomach grinds food. The legs move the body from one place to another. This movement is done by groups of special cells called *muscle tissue*.

There are three kinds of muscle cells, each doing a different job for the whole body. The large muscles are called *skeletal* or *voluntary* since one can decide to move them. *Smooth muscles* are those one cannot control. They are in the walls of the stomach, intestine, blood vessels, and other organs. The third kind of muscle tissue (*cardiac*) is found only in the HEART. Muscle cells can get shorter and fatter (*contract*) or stretch out long (*relax*). This shortening and lengthening causes parts of the body to move.

Skeletal muscles are the large muscles that one can control at will. They are consequently called *voluntary* muscles. Almost all of them are attached to the bones in the body by *tendons* which are composed of white fibrous CONNECTIVE TISSUE. Each muscle cell or fiber is long, tapering, and contains several nuclei. Many fibers form a bundle which in turn make up a muscle, such as the one in the upper arm called the *biceps.* Voluntary muscles possess dark and light bands or *striations.* These give a ladder-like appearance to the microscopic view of this muscle. *Striated* (voluntary or skeletal) muscles make up the bulk of the body.

Smooth muscles lack striations and are involuntary. One cannot decide to move them. They do so automatically under the control of the AUTONOMIC NERVOUS SYSTEM. They are found in the walls of most of the hollow organs of the body—digestive, respiratory, circulatory, urogenital systems, and in certain other places. "Goose flesh" on the skin is caused by minute smooth muscles. The spindle-shaped cells are much simpler in structure and function. Usually they are arranged in layers, one going around the organ (*circular*) and others going lengthwise (*longitudinal*). These cells have only one nucleus. The muscles contract and relax slowly and smoothly unlike most skeletal muscles.

Cardiac muscle is found in only one organ of the body, the heart. It is a really special tissue. It is striated like skeletal muscles yet functions smoothly and without willful control as in involuntary muscles. The long cells of cardiac tissue are joined together by CONNECTIVE TISSUE. This forms a fibrous network that causes the heart to work as one unit. H. J. C.

SEE ALSO: ANATOMY, HEART, HISTOLOGY, MUSCLE SYSTEM

## Muscular dystrophy (MUSS-kue-luhr DISS-truh-fee)

Muscular dystrophy is a rather rare disease that makes the muscles weak and useless. The visible signs of the disease (weakness and clumsiness) may resemble those of nervous disorders. But in muscular dystrophy the defect occurs in the muscles themselves and not in related structures.

The disease (which is often hereditary) causes muscles to become soft. There may be shrinkage of muscle tissue *(atrophy)* or enlargement *(hypertrophy).* Progressive muscular dystrophy leads to the relative uselessness of most muscles. J.M.C./E.S.S.

SEE ALSO: ATROPHY, HYPERTROPHY, MUSCLE SYSTEM, MUSCLE TISSUE

**MAKING SPORE PRINTS**

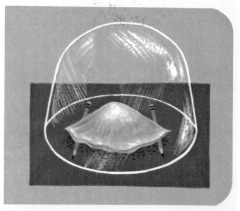

**Mushrooms reproduce by spores. One of the methods used in mushroom identification is making spore prints. A variety of mushrooms may be collected from damp wooded areas or marshy regions.**

1  **Remove the stipe or stalk from each mushroom. Spread a film of glue over a piece of cardboard. Rest the pileus or cap of the mushroom on two pencils over the cardboard. Put a plastic dish over this.**

2  **Spores will fall and stick to the glue. Use contrasting colors of cardboard depending upon spore color.**

**Mushrooms** Many mushroom plants look like umbrellas. They do not have CHLOROPHYLL, so they must get their food from other living or dead things. On the underside of the cap are little folds. These are called *gills* and contain the *spores,* the minute cells which grow into more mushrooms. A warm damp place is most favorable for mushroom growth.

**Mushrooms are fungi with caps, stems, and gills**

Courtesy Society For Visual Education, Inc.

**Russula, a flat-capped mushroom**

Mushrooms lack roots but develop a network of branches (*mycelium*) which serves as an attachment to the host it is living on. Mushrooms lack true stems so the handle of the umbrella serves as a supporting structure to hold the cap (*pileus*) up in the air. This is the fruiting body or *sporophore* which reproduces for the plant. It dies back after spore production but the mycelium may live for years periodically sending up a new crop of mushrooms when conditions are favorable. This explains what is sometimes called a *fairy ring,* a ring in the grass that seems to have been lightly trodden by feet. The story is told that this is where the fairies have danced. The mushroom spores have moved outward, forming this ring, to find more favorable soil.

Among the most delicious mushrooms are the MORELS. Many *puffballs* are edible if collected when they are very young and the flesh is firm and white. The *sulfur* mushroom is a bright yellow shelf fungus usually growing around the trunk of a dead tree. The *inky cap* variety drips black fluid which helps distribute the spores. The *Jack-O-Lantern* mushroom is bright orange and glows at night.

Most poisonous mushrooms belongs to the genus *Amanita*. The genus is characterized by a ring around the stem, by a cup of poison at the base of the stipe, and by the production of white spores.

Collecting edible mushrooms is risky for the amateur. There is no simple method for separating poisonous species from edible species.      M. D. F.

SEE ALSO: FUNGUS; PLANTS, CLASSIFICATION OF

**Brick top, one of many colorful mushrooms**

## Musical instruments

**Musical instruments** Musical instruments have a history as old as mankind. Many of the instruments now used in bands and orchestras have been developed from some of these very old instruments. Scientifically, musical instruments are divided into groups. The groups are named according to how the musical sound is produced or, to use scientific terms, how a series of *vibrations* is produced. Musical sound is produced on *stringed* instruments by bowing, plucking, or striking the strings. In *flute* and *organ* types of instruments, vibrations which create musical sounds are made by air being blown across a sharp edge. Small wooden reeds are used in the mouthpieces of *woodwind* instruments. They are set in motion and produce vibrations when the player blows into the instrument. *Brass* instruments produce music when they are blown with stiffened lips. Vibrations set up by striking different surfaces are produced on *percussion* instruments. The newest types of musical instruments are *electronic* instruments.

Each instrument has a characteristic sound dependent not only on the device which sets it vibrating but also on its shape, size, and the material from which it is made.

*Stringed instruments:* In these instruments, the vibrating string is the basis for musical sound. The *pitch* or *frequency* (vibrations per period of time) is dependent upon the length, thickness, and tightness of the string. *The greater the frequency, the higher the pitch.*

Short, thin strings produce fast vibrations resulting in high sounds. Long, thick strings vibrate more slowly and produce low sounds. If the vibrating part of a string is cut in half, the frequency, or number of vibrations, is doubled. If the stress on a string is increased four times, the frequency or pitch is doubled.

The piano is a good example of these frequency factors. There are short, thin strings for high notes and long, thick strings for low

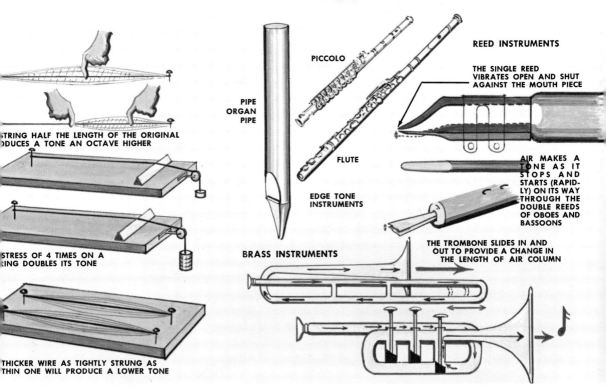

**PIPE ORGAN PIPE**

**PICCOLO**

**FLUTE**

**EDGE TONE INSTRUMENTS**

STRING HALF THE LENGTH OF THE ORIGINAL PRODUCES A TONE AN OCTAVE HIGHER

STRESS OF 4 TIMES ON A STRING DOUBLES ITS TONE

THICKER WIRE AS TIGHTLY STRUNG AS THIN ONE WILL PRODUCE A LOWER TONE

**REED INSTRUMENTS**

THE SINGLE REED VIBRATES OPEN AND SHUT AGAINST THE MOUTH PIECE

AIR MAKES A TONE AS IT STOPS AND STARTS (RAPIDLY) ON ITS WAY THROUGH THE DOUBLE REEDS OF OBOES AND BASSOONS

**BRASS INSTRUMENTS**

THE TROMBONE SLIDES IN AND OUT TO PROVIDE A CHANGE IN THE LENGTH OF AIR COLUMN

**The characteristic sound of a musical instrument is due to the way in which the sound is produced**

notes. The tone of each string is regulated by tightening or loosening it.

The stringed instruments heard in an orchestra are the violin, viola, cello, bass viol, and harp.

*Wind instruments:* Instruments in which columns of air are made to vibrate and produce musical sounds are called wind instruments. Vibrating air can produce tones of great power, variety, and beauty. Edge-tone, woodwind, and brass instruments fall into this category.

*Edge-tone instruments:* One of the earliest edge-tone instruments was a small flute made of bamboo or bone. It played only one note. Our modern flutes and piccolos will play many notes. Their pitch is controlled by opening and closing specifically placed holes on the front of the instrument. This is done by pressing down on metal levers called *keys*. Keys change the length of the vibrating column of air. The pitch can also be regulated by increasing the force of air being blown into the instrument.

The pipe organ operates on this same principle. It has many pipes of different lengths and sizes. The air that is forced across the lip of each pipe is controlled by valves called *stops*. These stops are pulled out or pushed in to regulate the length of the vibrating column of air.

*Woodwind instruments:* If you hold a blade of grass between your fingers and blow on it,

it will make a shrill tone. People of ancient times put a reed into a short bamboo pole to make a primitive reed or woodwind instrument. These instruments are the ancestors of our modern woodwind instruments. All woodwinds have either single or double reeds. The player blows over or through the moistened reed and into the instrument to set up a vibrating column of air. The rate of vibration is controlled by lip pressure on the reed. The pitch is changed by pressing keys that open and close on the front of the instrument.

Some of the woodwinds heard in orchestras and bands are the clarinet, oboe, English horn, bassoon, and saxophone.

*Brass instruments:* Brass instruments are made up of various lengths of tubing curved into a variety of shapes. When air is blown into the instrument, the lips of the performer act as a double reed. Valves on the front of the instrument are used to shorten or lengthen the column of air. Tones are controlled by the tightness or looseness of the lips (embouchure) and the breath of the performer.

Some of the brass instruments found in orchestras and bands are the trumpet, trombone, French horn, and tuba.

*Electronic instruments:* Electric guitars employ electric current and electronic circuits to amplify tones which have been mechanically produced. In the electric organ, the current and circuits produce, control, and amplify tones. A series of electronic disks are

✳ **THINGS TO DO**

**CONSTRUCTING YOUR OWN RHYTHM BAND**

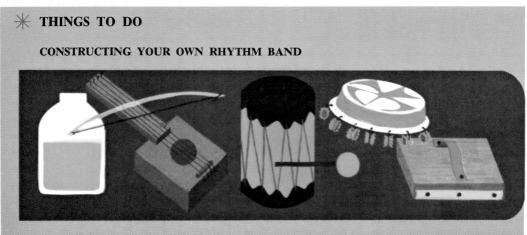

1 Musical bottles: Find eight bottles the same weight and size. Leave one empty. Put varying amounts of water in the others so the column of air left in each bottle can be tuned to a note of the musical scale. A stick may be used to tap each bottle. Which makes the high note? The lowest note?

2 Violin: Cut a large hole in the cover of a cigar box. Fasten a strip of wood on one end with screws. Fasten 4 small eye screws on the top end of this board and on the side of the other end of the box. Attach 4 pieces of picture wire across the violin to these screws. They may be turned in order to loosen or tighten the wires while tuning your violin. A small piece of wood should be inserted under the wires near one end of the box. A bow may be made from a curved stick and several long strands of hair.

3 Series of drums: Remove both ends from 1 pound (.45 kilogram) and 2 pound (.9 kilogram) coffee cans, and a large potato chip can. Cut circles of tire tubing about 2 inches (5 centimeters) larger than the open ends of the drums. With heavy cord or leather thongs lace the circles over the ends of the cans by following the illustrations. The drums may be hit with the hand or a beater made with a dowel rod inserted into a solid rubber ball.

4 Tamborines: Wire two bottle caps back to back. Fasten pairs of these to the rim of an aluminum pie pan. They will add "music" to your rhythm band.

5 Sand blocks: Tack a strip of sand paper to wooden blocks. Fashion a handle for the top. Use different coarseness of paper for each set to vary the sounds.

rotated in an electromagnetic field by a constant-speed electric motor. The frequencies generated in this way provide a wide variety of tones. The standard electric organ is equipped with two manuals and a pedal keyboard.

The human VOICE is the most versatile and personal of all musical instruments. It can express a variety of tones, qualities, and emotions. It is produced by a pair of mucous membranes or vocal cords. They are set into vibration by air from the lungs and act as a double reed. Air passes through as the opening between them widens or narrows. The tone color, quality, and depth of the voice depend on the size and shape of the cords and resonating cavities. These cavities are the windpipe, back of the throat, roof of the mouth, and sinus cavities.     T. L. L.

SEE ALSO: ELECTRONICS, SOUND

**Musk** Musk glands are common in the deer family. An abdominal one in musk deer is used in perfumes. Many such glands occur on legs and between hooves. They aid in locating resting spots.

**Musk ox** see Oxen

**Muskmelon** see Melon

**Muskrat** A muskrat looks like a huge, long-haired mouse. This large rodent is about 12 inches (30 centimeters) long and has a long, flat, hairless tail. It has a round head, little ears, and webbed hind feet. Muskrats get their name from their strong musky odor. They seem to love the water and are excellent swimmers and divers. Their bodies are kept warm and dry by two layers of thick fur. The undercoat is soft and silky. The outercoat consists of long shiny brown and gray hairs.

During the winter muskrats live in large dome-shaped huts which they build in swamps or in burrows which they dig on shore. They build the huts, which are about

J. W. Thompson
**A muskrat in danger can dive to its hut**

5 feet (1.5 meters) wide and 3-4 feet (.9-1.2 meters) high, from roots, stems, twigs, and mud. Each hut has two rooms or chambers, one above water and one underwater. The muskrats enter their huts through underwater tunnels, swimming in and out under the ice. The burrows dug in the banks have one chamber with many underwater tunnels.

During the summer muskrats build simple grass nests. Here their babies are born. Mother muskrats have from three to thirteen babies at one time, and they may have as many as five litters each year. Muskrats eat water plants, frogs, fish, vegetables, insects, worms, and shellfish.

Muskrat FUR, because of its long-wearing quality, is used in making fur coats. Muskrat flesh is called *marsh rabbit* when it is sold as meat.                                     D. J. A.
SEE ALSO: RODENTIA

Buchsbaum
**Blue mussels live in salt water**

**Mussel** The mussel is a two-shelled animal in phylum *Mollusca*. It looks like an OYSTER. The two halves of the shell are usually the same, hinged together to open so the animal can burrow into sand or mud for food.

There are two families of mussels. The salt-water mussels of family *Mytilidae* live on the ocean floor or attached to rocks with thread-like appendages. It is sometimes used as food. The inside of the shell is purple and pearl-like.

The fresh-water mussels of family *Unionidae* live in shallow inland shoals. They are not edible, but the lining of the shell has value for making "pearl" buttons. Both types of mussels have been known to produce an inferior pearl.                                     J. D. B.
SEE ALSO: MOLLUSCA, PEARL

**Mustang** A mustang is a wild or partly-wild small HORSE of the western United States. The mustangs are descendants of the horses brought over by the Spanish conquerors. They have been tamed and used as ranch horses.

**Mustard** The yellow or brown seeds of some of these annual HERBS are used for flavoring. LEAVES may be used in medicine. Still other species of mustard are pesky weeds in grain fields. FLOWERS are small and usually yellow. The FRUIT is dry.

Black mustard, from 2 to 6 feet (.6 to 1.8 meters) tall, forms large base leaves, which are serrated, lobed, and alternate. Fruit is less than an inch (2.5 centimeters) long. White mustard has lighter-colored fruit and larger seeds. Both kinds are used in condi-

The mustard plant and its seeds

The myna eats both insects and plants

ments. When water is added to ground seed an enzyme, *myrosin,* changes gluoside to a volatile oil containing sulfur.

The mustard flower is perfect and regular. It has four petals and sepals, six stamens, and one pistil of two carpels. The dehiscent fruit is classified as a silique. Mustard is a member of the family Cruciferae.      H. J. C.

SEE ALSO: CABBAGE

**Mutation**  A mutation is a new characteristic which appears suddenly in an organism and makes it different from its parents. It is caused by a change in a GENE or CHROMOSOME and can be inherited.

SEE: HEREDITY

**Mutism**  (MEW-tizz-uhm)  A small number of children, perhaps one in six thousand, are born deaf. These children are *mute*—unable to learn to speak without proper training. A defective LARYNX or voice box can also cause mutism.

Electronic devices now give speech to those who have a malfunction of the larynx.

The easiest form of communication to learn is the sign language, an elaborate system of manual gestures and finger spelling, invented for the deaf mute.      V. V. N.

SEE ALSO: DEAFNESS

**Mutualism** see Balance of Nature

**Myelitis**  (my-el-EYE-tis)  Myelitis is a Greek word having two meanings. In one sense, it means the inflammation of the *marrow,* the soft, spongy part in the center of a body organ. This is infection of the bone marrow called *osteomyelitis.*

A second meaning of myelitis means inflammation of the *myelin* sheath of a nerve fiber. The myelin is the outer covering of a nerve. Infection here can cause paralysis of the muscle supplied by the nerve.      B. M. H.

SEE ALSO: POLIOMYELITIS, NERVOUS SYSTEM, SPINAL CORD

**Myna**  The myna, or *mynah,* is a beautiful, wine-brown, tropical bird of Southeast Asia and the Pacific Islands. It belongs to the STARLING family. It is noted for its ability to mimic human speech. Because it is very friendly and fearless, it makes a good pet.

SEE: PARROT

**Myopia**  see Nearsightedness

**Myriapod**  see Centipede, Millipede

**Myrtle**  This is a common name for certain flowering plants in several different families. Many are evergreen.

Wax myrtle has gray-white FRUIT with a layer of fat which is used in soap and candles. Running myrtle is a ground cover with purple flowers. Shrubs by this name have white or rose FLOWERS and dark-blue berries. California laurel is called Oregon myrtle.      H. J. C.

SEE: PLANTS, TROPICAL; PROPAGATION

Myrtle has small pink or white flowers

**Myxedema**  Myxedema is puffiness or swelling of the tissues, especially around the eyes and legs. It is one of the symptoms of *hypothyroidism* (poor function of the thyroid gland). Infants with this disease are called *cretins.* They often have a large, protruding tongue, and will be severely retarded unless given thyroid hormone.      E.S.S.

SEE: CRETIN

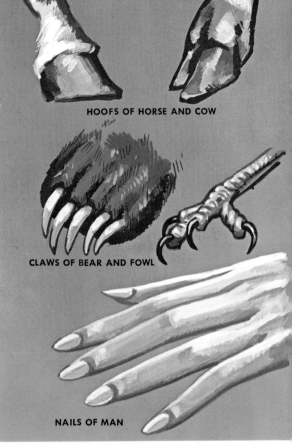

HOOFS OF HORSE AND COW

CLAWS OF BEAR AND FOWL

NAILS OF MAN

How and where an animal lives, and the kind of food it eats depends on the kind of hoofs, claws, teeth, or nails the animal has

**Nadir** The nadir is that point in the heavens directly opposite to the ZENITH—the point exactly over one's head. It is therefore directly beneath where one stands—in a straight line with the zenith and the center of the earth.

**Nail** Nails, claws and hoofs are found at the end of the digits (fingers and toes). These are all produced by the skin. A hoof surrounds the toe. A claw is sharp and grows out from the end of a toe. Nails are the flattened claws of the highest order of mammals—*primates.* Animals in this order include monkeys, apes, lemurs and man.

Nails are composed of a substance called *keratin,* a horny material which protects and wears. They are modified reptilian scales consisting of a hard top plate, the *unguis,* and a softer under plate, the *subunguis.* The subunguis corresponds to the bottom (ventral) side of a claw. In nails, this region is much reduced.

The *crescent,* a whitish half-moon on the nail, lies over the *matrix.* Nails grow from the matrix, which is formed by the deepest layer of the epidermis, the *germinative layer.* Growth from the matrix is continuous unless it is seriously injured. A nail grows about ⅛ inch (3 millimeters) a month. A fold of thin skin called *cuticle* surrounds the nail. 　　　　　　　　　　J.C.K.

SEE ALSO: SKIN MODIFICATIONS

**Naphtha** see Petroleum

**Naphthalene** see Chemistry

**Narcissus** (nahr-SISS-uhs) This FLOWER grows from a bulb or underground stem. LEAVES are narrow. Flowers are orange, white, or yellow.

*Narcissus* is the genus name. One species, *jonquilla,* has a cluster of deep-yellow blooms. Daffodil, species *tazetta,* has a white or yellow trumpet flower. Species *poeticus* is white with an orange rim on the cup. The three sepals on narcissus are the same color as the three petals. Additional floral parts form the corona, or tube, in the center between the corolla and stamens. Narcissus belongs to the family Amaryllidaceae. 　　　　　　　H. J. C.

The narcissus is a popular garden flower
Courtesy Society For Visual Education, Inc.

**Narcotics** Narcotic drugs lessen the sensations of the body and relieve pain. Larger doses can cause users to go into a stupor, sleep, or coma. No one should use narcotics without a doctor's advice.

These drugs strongly inhibit many bodily activities, so certain laws regulate their use. Most narcotics are derived from OPIUM. Opium is a reddish-brown, gummy substance squeezed from the capsule of the POPPY plant. Most of the world's opium comes from China and other far eastern countries.

Narcotics are taken by mouth, smoked, or injected into a vein. If taken over a long period of time, a person may become dependent on the drug. When this happens, the dose must be increased to produce the same effect. Such a person quickly becomes a *drug addict.*

Opium is a mixture of chemicals called *alkaloids.* Chief among these are *morphine* and *codeine. Heroin,* a very powerful narcotic, is derived from morphine. Heroin produces addiction so rapidly that its manufacture and import into the United States is prohibited. It cannot even be obtained by a doctor's prescription.

When a heroin addict is suddenly deprived of his drug, he may suffer severe pains in his body. About 24 hours after the last dose the addict begins to yawn, his eyes and nose run, and he sweats and becomes anxious and restless. He has an intense craving for the drug, cannot sleep or eat, and may have severe muscular pains, particularly in the back. Treatment is accomplished by improving nutrition, giving sedatives other than narcotics, and using psychotherapy. Methadone is a legal drug that can be prescribed to take the place of heroin and then can gradually be discontinued.

Morphine is extremely useful in relieving the pain and anxiety of a heart attack or of a broken leg. Synthetic drugs, such as meperidine and demerol, are also effective.

An overdose of a narcotic will slow the metabolism of the body to the point of death.

Cocaine is produced from coca plants in South America. Cocaine is used as an anesthetic in medicine.               B.M.H.
SEE ALSO: MORPHINE, PHARMACOLOGY

**Narwhal** see Whale

The hardy nasturtium grows almost anywhere

**Nasturtium** (nahs-TER-shuhm) Nasturtiums are climbing, soft-stemmed (herbaceous) annuals with red, orange or yellow flower petals. There are five spurred petals with the three lower ones fringed toward the center of the flower. The leaves are large and circular in shape.

These plants are members of the same family as water cress. They climb by means of tendrils which are modified leaf stems or petioles. Spurs on the petals are *nectaries,* secreting the nectar that attracts insects and insures pollination. Leaves have *palmate* venation, veins entering at one point and spreading out. Horticulturists have developed many new varieties.               J. C. K.

**Natural bridge** When a large section of a limestone cave roof collapses and leaves a middle section standing, a *natural bridge* is formed. Natural caves in limestone regions are more often formed when a surface river drains into a fissure in the bedrock, moves underground a short distance, and then gushes out on the face of a cliff.

Courtesy Society For Visual Education, Inc.

**A natural bridge carved from rock by erosion**

Natural bridges are formed differently in the many sandstone layers of the western and northwestern United States. They result from both the EROSION of running water and the work of winds. Some natural bridges are formed as the result of wind erosion entirely, although these are fairly rare.      H. S. G.

Courtesy Society For Visual Education, Inc.

**Natural bridge forming a double arch**

**Natural gas**   Natural gas was formed millions of years ago by the earth's movement, tiny sea plants and animals, and sunlight. Natural gas has been found in underground rock cavities. It often seeps to the surface.

Gas was produced by the chemical action of small sea plants and animals. The movement of the earth's crust caused this material to be buried and subsequently to decay. Most natural gas consists mainly of METHANE, a combustible HYDROCARBON.

The deposits of natural gas are reached by drilling wells. Geologists are able to determine, by soundings and by rock formations, its approximate location. Fuel, gas, gasoline, ink, synthetic rubber, plastics, drugs, and dyes are some of the natural gas products.      P.F.D.

SEE ALSO: GEOLOGY, PETROLEUM

**Natural number**   see Algebra

**Natural resources**   The natural resources of Earth are the land and soil, water, forests, grassland, other vegetation, fish and wildlife, rocks and minerals, and solar and other forms of energy. There are two groups of natural resources—nonrenewable and renewable.

The *nonrenewable* natural resources, called *fund* or *stock resources,* are so-called because removal of them uses up the present supply at a rate far, far faster than the rate at which they develop again. Examples of this group are metallic ores, COAL, PETROLEUM, and stone.

*Renewable* natural resources, called *flow resources,* consist of living organisms and their products, and solar and atomic radiation. These are termed renewable since they can be renewed or replenished in nature relatively quickly. WATER is an example.

Some natural resources, however, are difficult to place in such groupings. Soil, for example, is often thought to be renewable since erosion and used up soil foods can be remedied rather quickly. But it may take thousands of years to renew the upper layers of the soil or to cover exposed bedrock. Water, which is also commonly renewable, may take many years to replace after being extracted by wells from deep waterbeds.

Trees are a valuable natural resource. They provide lumber, paper pulp, fruits and nuts, turpentine and rubber, and, in addition, they prevent erosion

Courtesy Society For Visual Education, Inc.

**MINERAL DEPOSITS**

**SUNLIGHT AND SOIL**

**ANIMAL LIFE**

**WATER**

The physical characteristics and distribution of natural resources on the face of the earth vary according to geographical locale and CLIMATE. The reasons for this wide variation include amount of energy received from the SUN, effects due to moisture and heat, and geological composition of the continents and islands.

Agricultural resources are found mainly in humid regions of moderate temperature. In cold climates, the land is frozen most of the year. In hot, humid regions, floods and storms make crop cultivation difficult.

Mineral resources are found all over the world. The United States has a few of the minor metals. It depends upon other nations for many of the nonrenewable resources it uses. At the present rate of consumption, it is believed that in the early part of the next century humans will have used up the world's reserves of oil and gas. The other fossil fuel, coal, will be available for another 200 to 300 years. Much fuel is wasted when one form of energy is changed into another. For example, only one-third of the energy potential of oil is used to produce electricity. The rest is lost as heat. Energy availability sets the whole pattern of how humans live. Natural resources will continue to diminish unless life styles change drastically. This is particularly true of the United States, which presently consumes over half of the world's supply of nonrenewable materials.

Even though much less is known about the natural resources of the ocean than of the continents, much of the existing resources, both living and mineral, have yet to be exploited.

Fresh water is extracted from desalted

sea water. Minerals, which were originally in solution, are precipitated to the ocean bottom or lie within rock beneath the water. It is supposed that large quantities of MANGANESE cover some sections of sea bottom. Several of the minerals not found commonly in land deposits, such as NICKEL, occur in these deposits.

Natural energy resources, such as the sun and water, are only beginning to be used.

Until this century, coal and oil were the main energy sources. But more and more attention is being given to harnessing the energy provided by water and the sun. In the future hydroelectric power and solar cells will be used as an important source of energy.

*Conservation* of natural resources deals with the rate, purpose, and efficiency of use. This includes preservation, restoration, reutilization and substitution of the natural resources. Federal, state, and local laws govern the conservation of water, soil, minerals, forests, and wildlife.        D.L.D.

SEE ALSO: AFRICA, ASIA AUSTRALIA, CONSERVATION OF NATURE, EARTH, ENERGY CRISIS, EUROPE, FORESTRY, FOSSIL FUELS, GEOGRAPHY, INTERNATIONAL CONTROL OF NATURAL RESOURCES, MINERAL, NORTH AMERICA, SEA WATER, SOIL TYPES, SOUTH AMERICA

**Natural science** see Biology, Botany, Chemistry, Physics, Zoology

**Natural selection** see Evolution

**Naturalist** A naturalist studies nature, especially plants or animals. His method is usually based upon actual observation, thus camera, field glass, and microscope are very useful to him.

**Nature** Nature is the term often used for the total of the forces which produce the forms of life and of matter. These forces seem to operate according to certain patterns, or laws; thus the laws are called "natural." Whenever anything happens which does not seem to be in keeping with these laws, the occurrence (phenomenon) is called "supernatural."

**Nausea** Nausea is a sick feeling in the stomach. It includes a lack of desire for food and a tendency to vomit.

**Nautical mile** The regular mile, or *statute* mile, is 5,280 feet (1,609 meters). The *international nautical* mile is 6,076.1033 feet (1,852 kilometers).

The nautical mile is used by ships and aircraft to measure distance. It represents a one-minute arc on a sphere representing the earth. There are 60 one-minute arcs in one degree on the sphere.

SEE: EARTH, MEASUREMENT

**Nautilus** (NAW-tuh-luhs) The nautilus is related to the OCTOPUS and the SQUID. The shells of octopi and squid are absent or very small. The nautilus has a well-developed one, with many septa, or walls, to divide it into rooms or chambers. The animal lives in the last one. A cord of tissue extends from the body through the septa to the top of the shell. This cord secretes gas to make the shell light.

The nautilus swims rapidly by ejecting water through a *syphon*. Its foot is divided into about 94 tentacles. These are ringed and have no suckers. They are used to capture prey. Tentacles are covered by a hood. When the body and tentacles are withdrawn into the shell, the hood closes the opening. The nautilus has four gills for respiration and an almost-closed circulatory system. Two branchial hearts send blood to the gills. Above the esophagus is a large ganglion or brain that sends nerves throughout the body. A beak tears food and a RADULA pulls it into the mouth. An esophagus, large crop, muscular stomach, and intestine complete the digestive tract.        J. C. K.

SEE ALSO: MOLLUSCA

**Nautilus submarine** see Submarine

The nautilus' shell protects it from enemies
Chicago Natural History Museum

Civil Air Patrol

**Modern navigators use instruments that locate positions accurately**

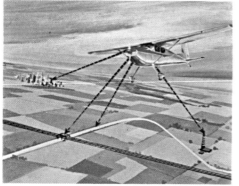

Civil Air Patrol

**A pilot may navigate by contact with known landmarks**

Civil Air Patrol

**Men on the ground can assist in navigating for an aircraft**

**Navigation** Navigation is the act of finding out where one is and selecting and following a pathway toward a goal one wishes to reach. Ocean vessels and large aircraft often have specially trained crewmen called *navigators*. These men work with a number of aids, including maps and charts, various tables and instruments, such as compasses and sextants. Radio and radar are electronic devices used.

Scientific navigation developed along with sea travel over many years. More recently, air and space travel have encouraged the invention and use of more and more precise electronic "guidance aids."

Aerial navigation differs from traditional water navigation in that a great deal more information is available from external sources. Ground support stations electronically feed navigational information to aircraft in flight. Automatic devices translate ground signals directly into information about position.

There are four main types of navigation. They are:
1. Pilotage
2. Dead Reckoning
3. Celestial
4. Electronic

The type of navigation that is used depends on many things such as the type and capabilities of the vehicle used, the time of day or night the trip is made, the weather conditions, and the training and skill of the navigator. Often more than one type of navigation will be used at the same time. This practice has the dual advantage of providing more precise navigation along with a greater margin of safety.

In *pilotage,* the navigator must have constant visual reference to his surroundings. He must be able to recognize familiar landmarks and proceed from one to the other. *Dead reckoning* requires much preparation and planning before a trip. Each leg of the trip is drawn on a chart. The length of each leg is determined as well as the true compass heading. The estimated time of travel is also determined for each leg. When possible, dead reckoning is often used in conjunction with pilotage. In years past, *celestial* navigation was a very important means of determining position. It is not used nearly as much today, however, except in some aspects of space travel.

As man travels farther, higher, and faster,

Compass direction and estimated distance enabled early navigators to deduce their position even during periods when sun and stars were not in view. Considering how primitive their equipment seems today, it is amazing how correct the sailors of old were on their courses

new and better means of navigation are vital. *Electronic* navigation is providing that means. Electronic devices, such as radio and radar, often working with computers, are making all-weather travel a reality. Transoceanic flights of jet aircraft and surface ships are now provided with precise information that allows them to pinpoint their position. On an experimental basis, electronic landing systems have been developed. These systems can land an aircraft without the direct aid of the crew.

Both radio and gyro compasses were developed, and the lead lines for measuring *depth* were replaced by the fathometer and the electronic echo sounder. In an airplane, this dimension in navigation becomes *height,* or *altitude,* and is computed by the instrument known as the ALTIMETER.

Clock-makers produced a finer time piece with less error called a *chronometer.* This clock is always set at Greenwich (London) time, which is Longitude 0°. The information about movements and positions of heavenly bodies in the official yearly almanacs is based upon Greenwich time. With the advent of radio, the Naval Observatory at Washington, D. C., began transmitting regular time signals for checking ships' clocks.

Measurements of speed are indicated by instruments named variously according to the craft in which they are located. An automobile has a *speedometer,* a ship has a *patent log,* and an AIRCRAFT has an *airspeed indicator.* As a ship or airplane travels, the forces of wind and current tend to take it off course. The navigator must keep a constant check on his position. Following years of using the astrolabe, the *marine* or *horizon sextant* came to be used in ships. The *bubble* sextant is used in airplanes.

In celestial navigation, it is assumed that at any given time, each star has some point on the earth's surface that is directly beneath it, called its *substellar point.* The navigator uses a compass and a sextant to measure the *direction* and angle of two stars. The exact time of each measurement is recorded with the *chronometer.* This information, supplemented by data from the *Nautical Almanac* and *Hydrographic Tables,* enables the navigator to compute his distance from the theoretical substellar point of each star. Using this distance as a radius, two circles may be drawn using each substellar point as a center. The exact position or *fix* is the intersection of the circles nearest to the dead-reckoning fix.

*Astro-navigation,* or navigation in outer space, is possible by using specific stars for reference points. During a particular mission the spacecraft "locks on" to a reference star to maintain its direction of flight, and then it points its antenna toward earth for a second reference. Satellites, in stationary orbits around the earth, are providing a highly accurate means for both ships and aircraft to determine their positions. Ships at sea are also guided by huge electronic navigational systems called *Sofar,* or Sound Fixing and Ranging. Many people and machines work day and night to guide travelers, whether on the sea or in space, to bring them safely to their destinations.

E.M.N.

SEE ALSO: ASTRONAUTICS, CELESTIAL NAVIGATION, DIRECTION FINDER, GYROSCOPE, INSTRUMENT LANDING SYSTEM, INSTRUMENT PANEL, MAP-MAKING, SHIPS, SPACE TRAVEL

**Neanderthal man** see Evolution of man

**Neaps** see Tide

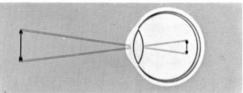

Courtesy Society For Visual Education, Inc.

If the light rays, or images, are focused in front of the retina of the eye, the person is nearsighted. The image can be made to focus on the retina by placing a concave lens in front of the eye

**Nearsightedness** Nearsightedness, also called *shortsightedness* or *myopia,* is caused by a defect in the shape of the EYE. People with myopia have eyeballs which are longer from front to back than the normal eye. They can see nearby objects without difficulty, but distant objects appear to be blurred to such people. Special glass or plastic lenses can correct the seeing difficulty.

The lens in the eye is similar in some respects to a camera lens because both gather in light rays reflected from objects and bring them to a focus upon a sensitive surface—the retina of the eye or film in the camera. However, while the camera lens can be moved closer to the film for distant objects and farther from the film for objects nearby in order to focus clearly, the lens in the eye cannot move back and forth within the eyeball, nor can the eyeball change in length in order to adjust.

The lens is held in position by the *suspensory membrane* and is attached to the *ciliary muscle.* When this muscle contracts, forcing the lens to become thicker and rounder, objects nearby are brought into focus. When it relaxes, the lens becomes flatter and distant objects are brought into focus. If the eyeball is too long, the lens can never become flat enough to compensate for the extra length, so the light rays entering the eye are brought to a focus before they reach the retina.

Eyeglasses with concave lenses can improve the vision of a person with myopia by bending the light rays in such a way that they can be brought into focus. Nearsightedness is believed to be an inherited defect.

B. J. C.

SEE ALSO: FARSIGHTEDNESS, OPTOMETRY

**Nebula** (NEBB-yuh-luh) The very early astronomers noticed that, in addition to the bright and sharp points of light they called stars, there were additional parts of the sky that looked like hazy, blurred patches. They called these patches *nebulae,* which meant "clouds." The light patches seen by these astronomers are much different from the clouds seen in the Earth's atmosphere.

Modern telescopes have shown that many of these clouds are really systems, or families of stars, that we know as GALAXIES. We now know that galaxies are millions of light-years apart and that the universe contains at least 100 million galaxies. Sir William Herschel, the famous eighteenth-century astronomer, termed these galaxies "island universes."

Of all of the nebulae that are galaxies of the universe, only one is visible to the naked eye—the Great Spiral in Andromeda. There are, however, other types of nebulae visible to the naked eye that are not galaxies. These are great clouds of cosmic dust that are spread throughout the universe. They are called *diffuse nebulae*. The brightest and best-known of these is the Great Nebula in Orion. Diffuse nebulae have no light of their own; their brightness is dependent on how close they are to a star. H. S. G.

SEE ALSO: GALAXY, SOLAR SYSTEM

**Nectar** In Greek mythology, nectar was the drink of the gods. IN BOTANY, it is the sweetish juice produced by many flowers. It attracts birds and insects that pollinate the flower. BEES use it to make honey.

SEE: POLLINATION

**Nectarine** The nectarine, which has been grown in Europe for at least 2,000 years, looks like a peach without down. There are *freestone* and *clingstone* types. The tree is similar to the PEACH tree. California produces many nectarines.

**The ascaris, a typical roundworm**

INTESTINE (OTHER ORGANS NOT SHOWN)

ANUS

TH

BODY WALL

**Néel, Louis Eugene** (1904-   ) The 1970 NOBEL PRIZE in physics was awarded to Eugene Néel and Hannes Alfven. Néel, a French physicist, was honored for his work on the magnetic effects of certain minerals. Dr. Néel's work investigating the possible uses of certain magnetic minerals called *ferrites* began in the 1930s.                          A.J.H.

**Negroid** see Evolution of man

**Nemathelminthes** (nemm-uh-thell-MINN-theez) Nemathelminthes are better known as "roundworms." Most of them are so small that they cannot be seen by the naked eye. Under a microscope they look very much like a piece of sewing thread. Nemathelminthes really means "threadworm."

There are many different species. They live in mud at the bottom of the ocean, in Arctic pools, in hot springs, in rivers, in moist soils, in deserts, and even in vinegar. Some prefer to live inside plants and animals where they cause disease. When a pet dog has "worms," it almost always has roundworms. There are about fifty kinds of roundworms which live in the bodies of people.

These worms make up one of the largest phyla of invertebrates. Next to the insects, there are more individual roundworms than there are in any other multicellular group. While most of them are under a millimeter, some grow to a length of 4 feet (1.2 meters). The female of the species is usually larger, often double the size of the male.

Moving from place to place is difficult for these worms. They have neither legs, like insects, nor bristles, like earthworms. By contracting and expanding a set of longitudinal muscles, they are able to move up and down, like waves. Others crawl by looping their bodies.

More than half the species live in soil or water. Since they cannot move quickly, they select soil rich in BACTERIA and algae. Others, successful as scavengers, live in deposits of decaying organic matter.

Many roundworms live as parasites in the bodies of living organisms. Since they rely solely upon the plant or animal to provide food, they will no longer have a home if they cause death to the host. They will also die if they are unable to find the right plant or animal.

Those which are parasitic on plants destroy about 1/10 of crops grown by American farmers. The plants wilt, are small in size, show leaf discoloration, and swell at the roots. Many roundworms attach themselves to the plant by piercing the roots and sucking the juices.

Those which are parasitic on animals often develop first in soil or water. The eggs of the HOOKWORM, for example, develop on the ground.

Some parasites move directly from one host to the next. The larva of the FILARIA worm, which causes swelling of the lymph glands, or elephantiasis, is passed from person to person by the mosquito. The larva of the TRICHINA worm, which lives in the muscles of scavengers like the pig and rat is passed on when one animal eats the flesh of another. In humans, this worm is brought into the body mainly by eating poorly-cooked pork.

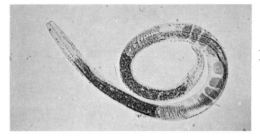

**Nematoda, a free-living marine roundworm**

The body of the roundworm is built on a simple "tube within a tube" plan. A hollow digestive tube is inserted into a larger outer tube which forms the body wall. The tubes are joined at the mouth and anus. The space between the tubes is a hollow cavity or "false coelom," since it is not lined entirely by the mesoderm, as is true in the coeloms of higher animals.

The roundworm has three body layers and there are organ systems for transportation between the various parts of the animal. While there are no circulatory or respiratory systems, there are simple excretory, nervous and reproductive systems.          E. P. L.

SEE ALSO: ANIMALS, CLASSIFICATION OF; ANNELIDA; PARASITE; PLATYHELMINTHES

**Nematocyst** (nee-MATT-uh-sist) A nematocyst is a stinging capsule found in some cells in the epidermis of certain animals, especially coelenterates. Poisonous fluid is secreted and discharged from the nematocyst through its thread-like end.

SEE: COELENTERATA, HYDRA

**Neodymium** (nee-oh-DIMM-ee-um) Neodymium, element 60, was discovered in 1885. It is a metal, slightly yellow in color, and belongs to the RARE-EARTH series of elements. The chemical symbol of neodymium is Nd.

Neodymium and the other rare earths are usually found together in nature.

*Didymium,* a mixture of neodymium and praseodymium, was once thought to be an element. The rare earths are so similar chemically that it is difficult to separate them. The atomic weight of neodymium is 144.24.
          J. R. S.

SEE ALSO: ATOM, ELEMENTS

**Neolithic** see Stone Age

**Neon** (NEE-ahn) Neon is one of the inert gases. Neon is element number

10 and was named from a Greek word meaning "new." Sir William Ramsey discovered it in 1898.

Neon is present in the air to the extent of about eighteen parts per million by weight. It is separated from the air by fractional distillation. Fractional DISTILLATION is the separation of the components of a mixture, like air, which have different boiling points by carefully controlled vaporization.

Neon lights are used in many advertising signs. Electricity is passed through the GAS and excites the electrons to a higher energy level. As the electrons return to the original level, light energy is given off. Neon lights give off an orange-red light.

The most unusual thing about the inert gases is that they usually do not combine or react with other elements. The outer electron shell is closed. Neon (symbol Ne) has an atomic weight of 20.183.          J. R. S.

SEE ALSO: ATOM, ELEMENTS

**Nephridia** (neh-FRIDD-ee-ah) Nephridia are tubules used to collect and excrete waste from the bodies of many kinds of animals. Wastes are collected from tissue fluids, blood, or body cavities. They are excreted or passed outside the body through a pore called a *nephridiopore*.

SEE ALSO: ANNELIDA, EXCRETORY SYSTEM

**Nephritis** (nef-RYE-tis) Nephritis is an inflammation of the kidneys. For many years, this was known as BRIGHT'S DISEASE. In this disease, the kidneys become swollen and cannot form urine. The body becomes filled with extra fluid, and the blood pressure may go very high. The disease occasionally follows a streptococcal infection of the throat that has not been properly treated with penicillin.

An allergic reaction to the streptococcus germ develops in the kidney, causing *acute* inflammation without actual infection. Examination of the urine will show albumin and red blood cells. With proper care, more than half of the acute cases recover without

# Neptune

permanent kidney damage. Unfortunately, a few cases go rapidly into a *chronic* form of nephritis. The kidneys become scarred with fibrous tissue and shrink to half size. They can no longer remove waste products from the blood. Uremia (kidney failure) develops.

Other forms of nephritis are caused by chemical poisoning, allergic reactions to blood transfusions, and crushing injuries to the kidneys. Sometimes there are thirty years between the acute nephritis attack and the last stage when uremia develops.

There are several ways of treating *renal* (kidney) failure. One is called *hemodialysis* (or the artificial kidney), where the patient's blood is passed through a cleansing machine for hours one or two times a week. Some patients are candidates for *transplants,* where a healthy *donor* kidney is surgically put into the ill patient *(recipient).* Transplants work well with identical twins, but are not as successful when the donor and recipient are not related because of *tissue rejection.*                                    E.S.S.

SEE ALSO: IMMUNITY

**Neptune** Neptune is one of the five outer planets that revolve about the sun. It is also one of the four planets known as the *giant planets.* Neptune is nearly the same size as URANUS and appears to resemble it in many other ways. Neptune is often referred to as the twin of Uranus.

Scientists believe that there is no life on Neptune. It is the eighth planet away from the sun and is too cold to support life. Neptune cannot be seen with the naked eye. It was not discovered until 1846. The remarkable fact about Neptune is that it was discovered by mathematical means and the laws of gravity, before it was ever seen through a telescope.

The story of the discovery of Neptune started with the discovery of Uranus. After astronomers had observed Uranus and had become convinced that it was a PLANET and not a star or a comet, they began to chart Uranus' orbit. They noticed that it seemed to speed up and then slow down as it trav-

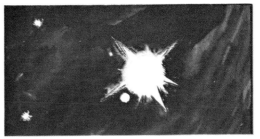

**Neptune and its inner satellite Triton**

elled around the sun. At first they thought they might be making mistakes in their figures and observations. Repeated calculations showed the same unusual differences. According to the laws of gravitation, some other heavenly body was exerting gravitational pull on Uranus to cause the change in its speed.

A young scientist in England, John Couch Adams, determined mathematically where the unknown planet ought to be. He wrote a letter to Sir George Airy, the Astronomer Royal. Airy did not pay much attention to the young unknown scientist. He could have pointed his telescope at the part of the sky that Adams had indicated, and he would have seen Neptune. He did not. At the same time, a French scientist, Urbain Leverrier, was working too. He solved the problem as Adams did and sent his information to Johann Galle, an astronomer in Berlin. The Germans had recently charted all the stars in that region of the sky. As soon as Galle received the letter, he looked for and saw the new planet. He was the first man to view Neptune and know it was a planet.

The orbital paths of Uranus and Neptune are roughly parallel. When Uranus begins to come up alongside Neptune, the gravity of Neptune pulls Uranus along and increases its speed. When Uranus passes Neptune, Neptune's gravity pulls Uranus back and slows it down.

Neptune's orbit is almost circular. Its average distance from the sun is about 2,793 million miles (4,493 million kilometers). It takes Neptune about 165 earth years to make a revolution around the sun. Its orbital speed is about 3½ miles (5.6 kilometers) per second. The diameter of Neptune is about 30,750 miles (49,487 kilometers). It has very low temperatures—from −350° F to −360° F (−201° C to −218° C).

Through a telescope Neptune looks like a small green disk. Because of Neptune's great distance from Earth, astronomers were not able to learn much about the planet using Earth-based telescopes. Two moons had been discovered and it was thought that the planet might have partial rings.

In 1989, the space probe *Voyager 2* visited Neptune and gave astronomers more data in a few days than had been gathered in centuries of observation. *Voyager 2* photographs revealed a beautiful blue planet streaked with high white clouds of frozen methane. Neptune's methane atmosphere has a feature called the Great Dark Spot, which is similar to the Great Red Spot of Jupiter. It is thought to be a rotating storm.

*Voyager 2* also gathered data on Neptune's temperature and magnetic field. Five complete rings were observed surrounding the planet, and six new moons were discovered. Neptune's largest moon, Triton, was found to have its own atmosphere. Because Triton has few craters, astronomers speculate that its surface is periodically renewed and reshaped by volcanic activity.          C.L.K.

SEE ALSO: SOLAR SYSTEM

**Neptunium** (nepp-TYOO-ne-um) Neptunium was first discovered by Philip Abelson and Edwin McMillan in 1940. It has 93 protons in its nucleus. It was the first *transuranium* element (following uranium) discovered.

There are fourteen isotopes of neptunium. Neptunium-224 has the shortest half-life of 4.0 minutes. Neptunium-237 has the longest half-life of $2.14 \times 10^6$ years. This isotope is available in small quantities and occurs in nature (in trace quantities).

Neptunium was first prepared by bombarding uranium with cyclotron-produced neutrons. It is currently obtained as a by-product of plutonium. It is chemically very active and has four oxidation states.     A.J.H.

SEE ALSO: ELEMENTS, NUCLEAR SCIENCE

**Nernst, Walther H.** (1864-1941) Nernst, a German scientist, physical chemist, was awarded the NOBEL PRIZE in chemistry in 1920 for important discoveries in thermochemistry.

Nernst specialized in thermodynamics. He studied the effects of high and low temperatures on chemical systems. He developed a heat theorem that became the third law of thermodynamics. His law stated that a substance in perfect equilibrium has zero entropy at a temperature of absolute zero.          A.J.H.

**Nerve cell** Nerve cells or *neurons* are found in the nervous system and help parts of the body work together. They also make an animal or man aware of what is happening in the outside world. For example, if one touches a hot stove, he jerks his hand back quickly. The hot stove is the stimulus, and the neurons, or nerve cells, in the nervous system are responsible for the quick action or response of the body muscles.

The cell body or *cyton* of the neuron is composed of a nucleus surrounded by *cytoplasm*. The neuron differs from other cells because *cytoplasmic processes,* or threadlike pieces, extend out from the cyton. On one side of the cyton are a number of short, rough, branched processes called *dendrites*. On the other side is a smooth process called an *axon* which is usually long.

The cyton does not have a cell membrane but is more dense around the surface of the cell. Irregular masses of darkly-staining material called *Nissl bodies* occur throughout the cytoplasm. They contain ribonucleoprotein (ribonucleic acid plus protein) in amounts depending on the physiological state of the neuron. Long, fine threadlike *neurofibrils* appear in the cytoplasm of nerve cells. Their function is unknown.

The nucleus in the cyton is round and has a definite nuclear membrane. Within the nucleus is a fine *chromatin* network concentrated around a spherical, darkly staining *nucleolus*.

The thick irregular-branching dendrites which extend out from the cyton contain Nissl bodies and most of the other bodies found in the cytoplasm. Since dendrites conduct nervous impulses toward the cyton, they are known as *afferent* processes. Some neurons, such as those with cell bodies in the *dorsal root ganglia* of the spinal nerves do not have dendrites.

Axons are smooth, often quite long, and usually unbranched except near their ends. They do not contain Nissl bodies. Some of

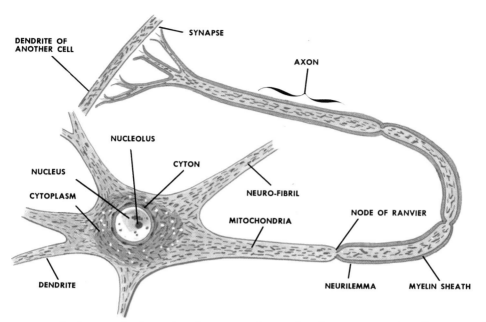

the neurons of the cerebral cortex have short, finely-branched axons. Because they carry impulses away from the cell body, axons are known as *efferent* processes. The cyton forms a cone-shaped extension at the point where the axon arises. This extension is known as the *axon hillock*.

Some axons have a sheath made of a lipoid (fatty) substance called *myelin*. Outside the myelin is a sheath of very flat cells with large nuclei. These are known as the *neurilemma* and form a supporting tube around the axon. Along the axon the myelin sheath is not continuous because the ends of the neurilemma cells dip down and come in contact with the axon. The points where the myelin is interrupted are called the *nodes of Ranvier*.

Some nerve fibers in the central nervous system have myelin sheaths but lack a neurilemma. Others are naked with no sheaths at all on the axons. In the autonomic system most of the axons lack myelin; some of them are naked and some have a neurilemma.　　　　　　　　J.C.K.

SEE ALSO: CELL, NERVOUS SYSTEM

**Nervous system** The nervous system helps an animal to find out about and respond to its surroundings or environment. Stimulations from the environment set up *impulses*. These travel over the nerves to the BRAIN or SPINAL CORD. The impulses are then sent through the nerves to the muscles needed for making the response. For example, if one's hand touches a hot stove, the hand jerks away. The heat is the *stimulus* and the jerk of the hand the *response*. When many muscles are used to respond to a stimulus, the nervous system *coordinates* them (causes them to work together).

### NERVE CELLS

The NERVE CELL or *neuron* is known as the structural unit of the nervous system, just as one brick can be called the structural unit of a brick wall. Most of the nervous system is composed of neurons, just as most of the brick wall is composed of bricks. Like all cells, the cell body of a neuron is composed of cytoplasm and a nucleus, but it is different from other cells because it has many projections. Short, rough, branching projections somewhat like the antlers of a deer are known as *dendrites*. There is one long smooth process with only a few branches known as an *axon*.

**HOW CLOSE ARE THE NERVE END-INGS ON YOUR SKIN? WHICH AREA IS MOST SENSITIVE?**

1 **Mark off circles on your skin on different parts of your body, palm, leg, abdomen, and top of foot.**
2 **Take a pointed knitting needle and press the point on the skin on various spots within each circle.**
3 **Each time try to determine if you feel pain, touch, hot, or cold sensations. Which areas of the body are most sensitive?**

Nerve cells occur in chains. The cells of the chain are not connected, but the dendrites of one cell touch, or are in contact with, the axons of the next. Impulses or messages sent to or from the brain travel along neurons. An impulse travels from the end of the axon of one neuron to the dendrites of the next neuron. The point at which the impulse passes from the axon end to the dendrites of the next neuron is called the *synapse*.

In addition to neurons, there are supporting cells in the nervous system called *neuroglia* cells. These are of different sizes, but they all have processes which extend around nerve cells and fibers. Some of these enlarge and remove (by *phagocytosis*) degenerating nervous tissue following an injury. It is thought that they may have a part in forming the *myelin sheaths* around the axons.

Axons of chains of neurons, grouped together side by side, make up both the nerves in the body and the tracts of fibers extending up and down or across the spinal cord and brain.

Cell bodies of neurons are usually grouped together. If the group is inside the brain or spinal cord, it is known as a *nucleus*. If the group is outside the brain and spinal cord, it is called a *ganglion*.

Messages or impulses coming to the spinal ganglia or to the brain nuclei are called *sensory* or *afferent impulses*. The nerves carrying them are called *sensory* or *afferent* nerves. In the same way, nerves carrying impulses away from ganglia and nuclei are called *motor* or *efferent impulses* and nerves.

The so-called mixed nerves entering the body from the brain and spinal cord are composed of both sensory and motor fibers.

REFLEX ACTS AND ARCS

The body will often make the same response in an involuntary way each time it receives a certain stimulus. This fixed pattern of behavior is known as a *reflex act*. The knee is jerked when a leg muscle tendon below the knee is stimulated by tapping. The tap stretches the muscle and stimulates the nerve endings or receptors in the tendon. Impulses are sent over sensory or afferent fibers to synapse with dendrites of motor cell bodies in the spinal cord. The axons from these cell bodies carry the impulses back to the leg muscle, which responds by contracting to its original length. This all occurs in a fraction of a second. The path that the impulses take from the muscle to the spinal cord and back to the muscle is called a *reflex arc*. Most reflexes are not so simple. They often involve synapses with several neurons in the cord and/or the brain. The muscles responding may not be those at the point of stimulation.

CENTRAL NERVOUS SYSTEM

The central nervous system is composed of the brain with its cranial nerves and the spinal cord with the spinal nerves.

The *brain* develops at the anterior or front end of the nerve cord, which is a thick-walled tube with a central cavity. At the posterior or back of the brain, the nerve cord develops into the spinal cord, and its cavity continues into the brain. Three bulb-like enlargements at the front end of the nerve cord give rise to all the adult parts of the brain.

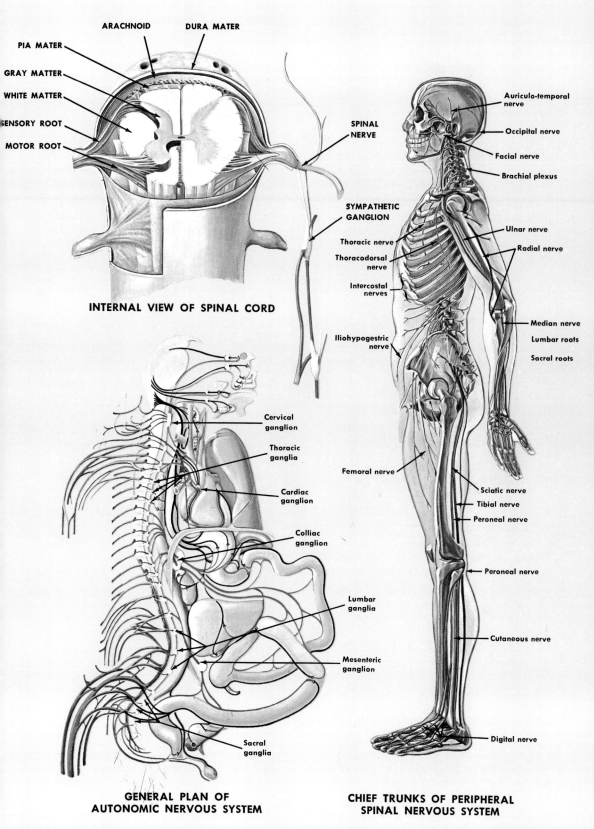

ARACHNOID     DURA MATER

PIA MATER

GRAY MATTER

WHITE MATTER

SENSORY ROOT

MOTOR ROOT

SPINAL
NERVE

SYMPATHETIC
GANGLION

**INTERNAL VIEW OF SPINAL CORD**

Auriculo-temporal
nerve

Occipital nerve

Facial nerve

Brachial plexus

Ulnar nerve

Radial nerve

Thoracic nerve

Thoracodorsal
nerve

Intercostal
nerves

Iliohypogestric
nerve

Median nerve

Lumbar roots

Sacral roots

Cervical
ganglion

Thoracic
ganglia

Cardiac
ganglion

Colliac
ganglion

Lumbar
ganglia

Mesenteric
ganglion

Sacral
ganglia

Femoral nerve

Sciatic nerve

Tibial nerve

Peroneal nerve

Peroneal nerve

Cutaneous nerve

Digital nerve

**GENERAL PLAN OF
AUTONOMIC NERVOUS SYSTEM**

**CHIEF TRUNKS OF PERIPHERAL
SPINAL NERVOUS SYSTEM**

©Denoyer-Geppert Co.

*Forebrain:* The first or anterior enlargement of the neural tube is called the *forebrain*. Constrictions soon divide the forebrain into two parts, the *telencephalon* and *diencephalon.*

Outpocketings on the sidewalls of the telencephalon become the region of the brain associated with the sense of smell. The telencephalon also forms stalk-like projections ending in cup-like disks. The disks lead to the retina of the EYE, and the optic nerves serving the eye grow out into the stalks.

Paired outpocketings on either side of the telencephalon form the *cerebral lobes.* In man the CEREBRUM with its highly-developed cortex is the largest part of the brain. It is associated with learned behavior. The lobes enlarge and fold back, covering most of the other areas of the brain.

The diencephalon connects to part of the PITUITARY gland and several other regions of the brain containing nuclei which have various functions. Some of these nuclei control reflexes in body organs (*viscera*) and blood vessels. Others serve as relay centers to the cerebrum for impulses which have to do with sight, hearing, and smell.

*Midbrain*: The second part of the brain, the midbrain, is the least changed of all three primary parts. Since it serves as the end-station for the optic tracts, its function is primarily visual. The third and fourth cranial nerves arise here and go to the eye muscles.

*Hindbrain:* The hindbrain forms the CEREBELLUM, pons, and MEDULLA OBLONGATA. The latter two structures plus the midbrain are the brain stem. The cerebellum consists of two hemispheres or lobes, and it serves to coordinate the action of muscles in voluntary responses. For example, the act of picking up a pencil is conscious and voluntary. It involves muscles in the fingers, forearm, upper arm, and shoulder. The cerebellum coordinates the muscles in an action. Most of the pons is composed of fibers connecting the two parts of the cerebellum with the cerebrum of the brain. The fifth cranial nerve, enervating the head parts, emerges from the pons.

The medulla contains fiber tracts connecting various parts of the brain and the spinal cord. Nuclei of most of the cranial nerves are located in the medulla.

### SPINAL CORD

In cross-section, the spinal cord consists of an H-shaped inner region of gray matter made up of cell bodies of motor neurons and fibers connecting different regions of the cord (*association fibers*). An outer region called the *white matter* is composed of bundles of axons and dendrites.

Between the vertebrae, thirty-one pairs of *spinal nerves* connect to the cord. Each nerve divides into a dorsal and ventral root before it joins the cord. The *dorsal roots* bear ganglia containing the cell bodies of the sensory fibers. The *ventral roots* contain motor axons coming from the cell bodies in the cord. The nerves themselves are mixed, receiving motor fibers from the ventral roots and conducting sensory fibers to the dorsal root ganglia. In the neck, shoulder, and hip regions, the ventral roots join to form networks (plexuses).

### AUTONOMIC SYSTEM

The autonomic system controls involuntary body functions, those which are accomplished without conscious effort. Gland secretion, digestion, heart beat, and blood circulation are examples. The autonomic system has two subdivisions, the sympathetic and the parasympathetic.

*Sympathetic:* The part of the autonomic system known as the sympathetic is centered along the middle part of the spinal cord. It contains both sensory and motor fibers. The cell bodies of the sensory fibers are in the *dorsal root ganglia.* Sympathetic efferent fibers run through the spinal nerves from the organs or viscera to nuclei in the cord. Sympathetic motor fibers arise from nuclei in the cord and run as *preganglionic* fibers through the spinal nerves to sympathetic ganglia located either near the cord or in the organs they enervate. In these ganglia, preganglionic fibers synapse with the cell bodies of *postganglionic* fibers.

*Parasympathetic:* The parasympathetic system is centered partly in the brain and partly in the *sacral,* or lowest, region of the spinal cord. Some of the cell bodies of sensory fibers and motor preganglionic fibers are located in the medulla. Preganglionic fibers run through the cranial nerves associated with the medulla to ganglia in the organs they supply. The afferent fibers run through cranial nerves to their nuclei in the medulla.

The parasympathetic afferent and motor fibers in the sacral region are arranged like those of the sympathetic division.

Most organs are enervated by both sympathetic and parasympathetic fibers, and their actions are opposite.　　　J. C. K.

SEE ALSO: AUTONOMIC NERVOUS SYSTEM, CELL, EMBRYOLOGY, MUSCLE SYSTEM

**Nests** see Bird nests

**False nettle**

**Nettle** Nettle is the name given to many plants in one family, the *nettle family,* especially those with small, stinging hairs. When these hairs touch skin, they produce small amounts of *formic acid* which can cause a rash.

**Neurohormone** see Atropine, Biochemistry

**Neutralization** Neutralization is a type of chemical reaction in which an acid and base exchange parts to form water and a salt. In complete neutralization, the resulting solution usually has neither acidic nor basic properties, and is called *neutral.*

An acid is a compound which in solution releases *positive hydrogen ions* ($H^+$) and a negative ion. Bases in solution release a *negative hydroxyl ion* ($OH^-$) and another positive ion.

In neutralization, the characteristic parts of an acid and a base, the hydrogen ion and the HYDROXYL ion, unite to form water. ($H^+$ plus $OH^-$ produces HOH or $H_2O$, water.) Thus the acid and base lose their abilities to act. The remaining parts produce a SALT, which is a substance that will separate to form positive ions other than hydrogen, and negative ions other than hydroxyl. Salts may be acidic or basic, but usually are neutral.

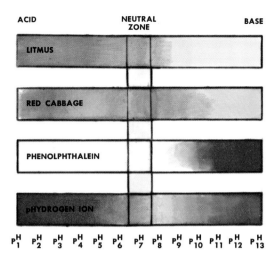

| ACID | NEUTRAL ZONE | BASE |
| --- | --- | --- |
| LITMUS | | |
| RED CABBAGE | | |
| PHENOLPHTHALEIN | | |
| PHYDROGEN ION | | |

$P^H_1$　$P^H_2$　$P^H_3$　$P^H_4$　$P^H_5$　$P^H_6$　$P^H_7$　$P^H_8$　$P^H_9$　$P^H_{10}$　$P^H_{11}$　$P^H_{12}$　$P^H_{13}$

Solutions range from acidic to neutral to alkaline. These indicators show acid-neutral-or-alkaline reactions of solutions by their color changes

Complete neutralization occurs when acids and bases of equal strengths are combined in equal amounts. A chemist knows when neutralization is complete by using indicators, such as litmus paper which changes color in the presence of acids or bases. Phenolphthalein is another commonly used indicator.

Neutralization occurs in many important processes of the human body such as digestion and metabolism. It is widely used in chemical analysis and in industry.　　J. K. L.

SEE ALSO: ACIDS AND BASES, CHEMISTRY

**Neutrino** (new-TREE-noh) This is an *elementary particle* emitted from atomic nuclei and predicted by Pauli to satisfy *conservation laws.* Reines proved it exists. There are two neutrinos and two antineutrinos. Each has only ENERGY and not mass or electric charge.

SEE ALSO: NUCLEAR ENERGY, NUCLEAR SCIENCE

**Neutron** (NEW-trahn) It is an elementary NUCLEAR PARTICLE, stable in atomic nuclei, unstable (HALF-LIFE 12 minutes) in free state. Its mass is 1838 ELECTRON masses. It has *no electric charge.* Neutrons and PROTONS are present in all *atomic nuclei* except HYDROGEN.

Neutrons were discovered in 1932 by James Chadwick, an Englishman. Chadwick identified the neutron as a particle given off by a RADIOACTIVE ELEMENT.

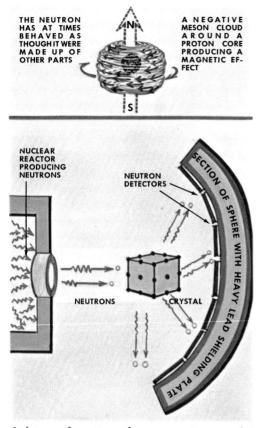

THE NEUTRON HAS AT TIMES BEHAVED AS THOUGH IT WERE MADE UP OF OTHER PARTS

A NEGATIVE MESON CLOUD AROUND A PROTON CORE PRODUCING A MAGNETIC EFFECT

NUCLEAR REACTOR PRODUCING NEUTRONS

NEUTRON DETECTORS

SECTION OF SPHERE WITH HEAVY LEAD SHIELDING PLATE

NEUTRONS

CRYSTAL

A beam of neutrons from a reactor are shot through a crystal. They give information about the position of the crystal's atoms and magnetic structure, depending on how they are scattered or refracted

Free neutrons are produced by the fission of elements such as uranium 235, by direct nuclear interactions as in cosmic RADIATION, or by high energy proton bombardment in cyclotrons. Neutron radiation penetrates deeply into human tissue. Therefore, nuclear bomb explosions are a great threat to mankind.

Neutrons freed by one of the above processes, disintegrate into a proton, electron, and neutrino, with a lifetime of about twelve minutes.

Neutrons, because of their electrical neutrality, are useful as "bullets" shot at the nuclei of atoms in nuclear experiments. Therefore, they are commonly used in studying the structure of matter. They also are used to start chain reactions in nuclear fission. J. K. L.

SEE ALSO: ACCELERATORS (PARTICLE); NUCLEAR ENERGY; NUCLEAR REACTORS; NUCLEAR SCIENCE; RADIATION, BIOLOGICAL EFFECTS OF

**Neutron star** A neutron star is a very small star. It is 10 kilometers (6.2 miles) to 20 kilometers (19.8 miles) in diameter. Made mostly of neutrons, this star has a very large density.

A star with a mass between 1.4 and 4 solar masses can form a neutron star. As stars age, their densities increase. When a star reaches a density of $10^{10}$ grams/cm$^3$, the electrons of atoms begin to combine with the protons of an atom to form neutrons. At this point, the star is a neutron star. This great density produces strong gravitational attractions that allows the star to rotate at high speeds. A.J.H.

**Newt** (NOOT) The newt is an amphibian which belongs in the same group with the SALAMANDERS. It is about 4 inches (10 centimeters) long, with four legs, and a strong round tail, which is used to help it swim. Some newts are bright red on top, yellow on the bottom, and have black rimmed scarlet dots along the sides. The newt feeds on snails, insects, and worms.

There are many different kinds of newts. They are found in Europe, Asia, and North America. Some newts live entirely in the water and some entirely on land, but most newts spend part of their lives on land.

They lay tiny eggs on the leaves of water plants. These eggs are laid singly. The newly-hatched newt does not look like its parent. It is a little tadpole that attaches itself to the leaf of a water plant. It breathes through gills. About three weeks after it hatches, the legs appear and lungs develop. After the newt has moved to land, it is called an *eft*. The adult newt, or eft, has a flatter tail than the other salamanders do. Newts have the power of REGENERATION,

The red eft lives on land as an adult

that is, if a leg is accidentally cut off, a new one will grow in its place.

In the fall, the little newt leaves the water and lives in damp places on the land. It continues to grow until it reaches the adult stage. It then turns a green color and returns to the water to seek a mate. In the spring, during the breeding season, the males become a very bright color and develop broad crests on their backs. Newts are easily raised in semi-aquatic aquariums.    W.J.K.

SEE ALSO: AMPHIBIANS, METAMORPHOSIS

**Newton, Sir Isaac** (1642-1727) Sir Isaac Newton was the great English natural philosopher who is best known for his important discovery of the laws of GRAVITY. In addition to these laws, he proved that a beam of sunlight, or white LIGHT, is composed of the seven colors of the rainbow: red, orange, yellow, green, blue, indigo, and violet. He did this by allowing a beam of sunlight to pass through a small hole into a darkened room and then through a prism.

Newton also invented a reflecting TELESCOPE for his own scientific study, and later built a similar one for contemporary astronomers to use. Although it was not the first reflecting telescope ever built, it was the first ever to be used in the study of astronomy.

Intensely interested in mathematics, Newton invented integral and differential calculus. In 1687 he published his great book *Philosophiae Naturalis Principia Mathematicae; or Mathematical Principles of Natural Philosophy,* a book which laid the foundations for the science of PHYSICS. It is interesting to note that Newton's poverty at the time forced him to allow his astronomer friend, EDMUND HALLEY, to bear the financial burden of publishing it.

In this book, Newton presented his theories and laws about the motions of objects and the forces producing and resisting these motions. For the first time, a mathematical basis was provided for understanding the motions of

Fenga-Donderi Collection
**Sir Isaac Newton**

the objects of the universe, whether they were planets and stars or baseballs and bats.

Newton's laws are the earliest statement of the relations of FORCE, mass, distance, and time. Much of the evidence Newton used to support his laws was based on observations of planets and comets. His laws help present-day scientists to put satellites into orbit around the Earth and other celestial bodies.

His identification of gravity, as an example of the mutual attraction that exists between all bodies, is commonly considered his most notable accomplishment. It is actually only one of many equally important contributions by Newton.

One of his first papers was on optics in which he discussed reflection, refraction, spherical lenses, lens grinding, lens errors, and color. His discovery that white light is composed of the colors of the rainbow disturbed many of his fellow philosophers.

Newton supported his theories with many experimental observations, all accurately recorded and well organized. His discoveries answered profound questions which had puzzled learned men for centuries. His theories disproved many old theories and thus were the cause of argument and debate.

Having been elected a fellow of the Royal Society at the age of thirty, Newton served as President of the Society for the last twenty-four years of his life, being re-elected each year. In 1705, when he was sixty-three, he was knighted by Queen Anne. He was also elected to membership in the French Academy of Science, a great honor, indeed. When he died on March 20, 1727, he was buried in Westminster Abbey, honored as one of the greatest men England had ever produced.    M. W. K.

**Niagara Falls** see North America

**Niche** (NICH) Niche is a term used by ecologists to describe the role or job of a plant or animal in its *habitat*. It is the lifestyle of a specie. Charles Elton, a British ecologist, coined the term.

Every niche in every natural environment in the world is filled by some living thing. No two species can occupy the same niche at the same time unless they are in different habitats. Certain bacteria and fungi have the role of decomposing. Green plants have the job of making sugar. Bees pollinate flowers. Some insects are scavengers. Lichen break up rocks into soil.

When an organism adapts to a specific niche, it cuts down on competition. This permits a more balanced ECOSYSTEM, allows for a greater variety of species, and a more efficient use of resources. An animal or plant that cannot find a niche becomes extinct. H.J.C.

**Nickel** Nickel is a very hard, magnetic, metallic element. It is almost silver-white. Nickel, capable of a high polish, does not rust easily. Its chemical symbol is Ni. Axel Cronstedt, a Swede, is credited with discovering nickel in 1751.

Nickel is seldom used in its pure form but is employed as an alloy with other metals. Since it provides an extremely hard surface, nickel is used in ELECTROPLATING. Certain types of electric batteries use nickel-alloy ELECTRODES.

Nickel-steel alloys are important in combining iron and steel into the strongest, toughest steels. Nickel is employed more in steel alloys than for any other purpose.

*Stainless steel* combines iron, chromium, and nickel. *Invar alloy* is used in measuring tapes and watch springs. *Alnico* is an alloy of aluminum, nickel, cobalt, and iron. Alnico magnets are more magnetic than steel magnets. Copper and nickel are merged into MONEL METAL. It is used in restaurant steam tables, kitchen sinks, and cabinets. Monel metal is easily kept bright and clean.

Nickel used to be alloyed with zinc in the United States five-cent piece. Now cheaper alloys are used. The richest nickel ores of the western countries are mined near Sudbury, Ontario, in Canada. Small but valuable deposits occur in Norway, Cuba, and Japan.

Nickel's atomic number is 28. Its atomic weight is 58.71. P. F. D.
SEE ALSO: ALLOY, ATOM, ELEMENTS

**Nickel-plating** see Electroplating

**Nicolle, Charles Jules Henri** (1866-1936) Nicolle, a French physician and bacteriologist, was awarded the 1928 NOBEL PRIZE in physiology and medicine. He worked with the transmission of the disease *typhus*.

Nicolle first observed typhus when he was in charge of the Pasteur Institute in Tunis. Typhus was common throughout the city, but no one had ever contracted it while in the hospital. Considering this fact, Nicolle realized that the only significant change to occur in the patient, upon admission to the hospital, was the removal of lice-infested clothing and a thorough washing. He correctly concluded that body lice must have been the carrier and transmitting agent of the typhus. P.P.S.

**Nicotine** (NICK-uh-teen) Nicotine is a natural chemical made in TOBACCO plants. It is poisonous and small amounts eaten or injected can cause severe nausea or death.

Pure nicotine is a clear liquid, but it becomes dark brown when exposed to air. Its formula is $C_{10}H_{14}N_2$. It has a burning, bitter taste. It is classed as an *alkaloid*.

Nicotine is used in INSECTICIDES and for studies of nerve and heart reactions. It is a hazard to smokers. D. A. B.

**Nictitating membrane** see Frog

**Night** see Day and night, Earth

**Night-blooming plants** Most plants bloom in daytime and many close at night. But night-blooming flowers open at night and close in bright sunshine. Most night-blooming flowers are of tropical origin. They are most often white and are usually very fragrant.

The best known night-blooming plant is the night-blooming *cereus*.

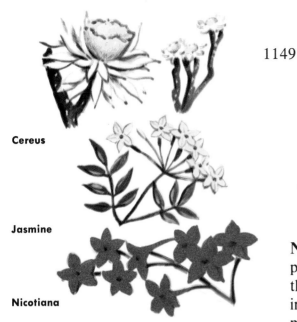

**Cereus**

**Jasmine**

**Nicotiana**

European nightingale

Other plants may bloom for several nights, as do the night JASMINES. Many tropical plants will bloom for several nights, but they are not commonly cultivated. Some plants bloom during the latter part of the day but their flowers are at their finest at night, and they are most fragrant after sundown. Some flowers bloom during the day if the weather is cloudy and overcast.

Plants belonging to the genus *Nicotiana* are the most outstanding of the hardy garden flowers that bloom after sunset and at night. They have clusters of sweet-smelling flowers that open in the evening or on sunless days. The easily raised evening primroses are also popular garden night-blooming plants. Others are evening campion, NIGHTSHADE, evening star, evening stock, FOUR-O-CLOCK, night phlox, akebia quintas, gladiolus tristis, hemerocallis thunbergi, and hesperis. M. R. L.

SEE ALSO: PLANTS, TROPICAL

**Nighthawk** The nighthawk is a goatsucker related to the whippoorwill. It has mottled brown feathers and a short, wide beak to catch insects in flight during the night. It makes a booming call during its dives.

Nighthawk

**Nightingale** The nightingale is a European bird related to the American thrush. It is a small bird, about 6½ inches (16.5 centimeters) long, with a pale brown breast and reddish-brown wings. The tail is a bright russet. The male sings day and night and its song is famous for its variety.

There are two species of nightingale, one of which ranges from Britain across southern Europe to Asia and another which does not reach western Europe. Both winter in northern Africa, migrating north in April. The males arrive before the females.

The nightingale nests in thick brush. The nest is cup-shaped, lined with fine roots and balanced in the undergrowth. From four to six dark olive eggs are laid. The birds feed on insects and worms. E. R. B.

SEE ALSO: THRUSH

**Nightshade** see Wild flowers

**Nimbo-stratus** see Clouds

**Nimbus** see Clouds

**Niobium** (nee-OH-bee-um) Niobium is a shiny, grayish metallic element. It was discovered in 1801 by Charles Hatchett. Its original name was *columbium*. This name is still used often in talking about its minerals.

It was recently discovered that niobium can withstand very high temperatures. It melts at 2,468° C. (4,474° F.). It promises to be important in high temperature alloys and stainless steel for airplanes and rockets.

Niobium (symbol Nb), element number 41, has atomic weight 92.906. J.R.S.

**Niter** see Saltpeter

**Niton** see Radon

**Nitrate** Nitrate is a SALT or ESTER of nitric acid. The nitrate compound contains nitrogen, oxygen, and some other element. Nitrates are used in the manufacture of medicines, photographic solutions, fireworks, fertilizers, and NITRIC ACID. Any nitrate contains a ($NO_3$) radical.

**Nitration** Nitration is the substitution, by means of a chemical reaction, of an ($-NO_2$) group for a hydrogen atom or other atom in a molecule. Nitric acid is commonly used as the source of the ($NO_2$) group.
SEE: CHEMISTRY

**Nitric acid** Clear, fuming, corrosive nitric acid acts readily upon metals and organic matter. It mixes with water, and is a good conductor of electricity. It can be prepared by oxidation of ammonia.

**Nitrogen** (NYE-troh-juhn) Nitrogen is an element found in plants, animals, air and other non-living compounds. About 78% of the atmosphere is made up of nitrogen gas. It is colorless, odorless and tasteless. Nitrogen (symbol N) is element number 7. Its atomic weight is 14.007.

Nitrogen gas is difficult to dissolve in water and does not combine readily with most elements. It is very essential for both plant life, which uses nitrogen to grow, and animal life, which uses nitrogen in very complicated structures called PROTEINS.

Nitrogen was first mentioned in writings by D. Rutherford in 1772. Later it was studied by Scheele and LAVOISIER and at that time was called *azote*. The word *nitrogen* comes from the Greek word *nitron* or *saltpeter,* a common compound of nitrogen. Most of the supply of soluble nitrogen once came from SALTPETER or potassium nitrate, $KNO_3$. The supply was limited until large amounts of Chile saltpeter, or sodium nitrate, $NaNO_3$, were discovered in northern Chile. Some other sources of nitrogen are coal and animal residue.

Nitrogen in the laboratory is prepared by heating ammonium nitrite, $NH_4NO_2$;
$$NH_4NO_2 \rightarrow N_2 + 2H_2O$$
In industry nitrogen is prepared by liquefying air. Nitrogen turns to a liquid at a temperature of about -196° C. (-320.8° F.), the boiling point of nitrogen.

Nitrogen gas is quite inert and combines with other elements very slowly. The reason is that the atoms in the diatomic molecule of nitrogen, $N_2$, have a very strong bond. However, when nitrogen does combine with other elements, it forms some of the most active compounds. For example, EXPLOSIVES such as NITROGLYCERIN and trinitrotoluene, or TNT, are nitrogen compounds.

AMMONIA gas is an important compound of nitrogen. In the laboratory it is made by adding a strong base to an ammonium salt:
$$NH_4Cl + NaOH \longrightarrow NH_3\uparrow + NaCl + H_2O$$
In industry ammonia is produced by the Haber process.

Other compounds of nitrogen are nitric acid, nitrous acid, nitrogen dioxide, nitrous oxide or "laughing gas," as well as many organic compounds.                E. Y. K.
SEE ALSO: ELEMENTS, HABER PROCESS

**Nitrogen cycle** Most nitrogen found in the body is in the form of proteins which contain mainly CARBON, HYDROGEN, OXYGEN, and NITROGEN. Humans and animals cannot get the necessary nitrogen directly from the air or soil. They get nitrogen from plants and from other animals which have eaten plants.

The excretion of animals, electrical discharges in the atmosphere, nitrogen-fixing BACTERIA, and saprophytic bacteria all help in making the cycle of nitrogen complete.

Nitrogen released by animals in the form of AMINO ACIDS, UREA, and other nitrogen wastes, is attacked by bacteria that use ammonia as a fuel to produce energy. In this process oxidation takes place and nitrites are formed. In the same manner nitrate bacteria combine oxygen with nitrites

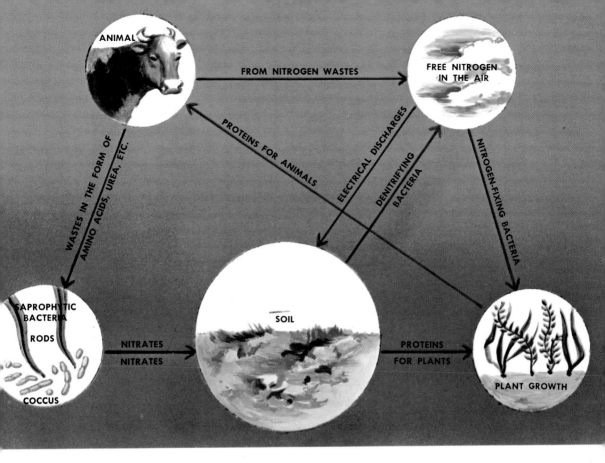

to form nitrates. This nitrate in the soil is then available for plant life to absorb and use. Animals eat the plants and change plant protein to animal PROTEIN.

Electrical discharges in the atmosphere help combine nitrogen with oxygen to form nitrates, which are added to the soil by rain. Nitrifying bacteria which attack decaying plants, animals, and wastes also enrich the soil with soluble nitrogen compounds. Some nitrogen is lost to the air by burning of organic matter and denitrifying bacteria which break down nitrates to release free nitrogen into the air.

Besides using FERTILIZERS man can help enrich the soil with nitrates by alternating his crops with a planting of a legume. Nitrogen-fixing bacteria attack the roots of legumes getting their nourishment from the roots, and in the process they use nitrogen from the ATMOSPHERE. The host plant develops growths called *root nodules* which house the bacteria. The bacteria are destroyed when the plant gets older and stronger, and in the process the plant digests the bacteria which are rich in nitrates. Some of the common LEGUMES are beans, peas, and alfalfa.                    E. Y. K.

SEE ALSO: CARBON CYCLE, ELEMENTS IN THE HUMAN BODY, SAPROPHYTES

**Nitroglycerin**    (nye-trow-GLIH-suhr-in) Pure nitroglycerin is a clear, syrupy liquid, so unstable that it explodes when jarred or put under sudden pressure. It is a medicine and a substance for industrial EXPLOSIVES.

Commercial nitroglycerin is a thick, yellowish liquid, formula $CH_2NO_3CHNO_3CH_2NO_3$. Since its discovery in 1846 by an Italian chemist, it presented man with the problem of its safe and wise use. Doctors know that certain circulatory ailments are relieved by use of capsule doses of it. A small amount of it burns harmlessly when lit in an open vessel. But when confined and jolted, it explodes with more than 20 times the heat and expansion of gunpowder.

ALFRED NOBEL in 1867 found that by mixing the syrupy liquid with clay, he could obtain a relatively stable form—*dynamite.* Another mixture is *cordite,* containing guncotton and nitroglycerin.                    D. A. B.

**Nitrous acid** Nitrous acid is a blue, unstable solution that breaks down to form brown nitrogen tetraoxide and nitric acid in solution. It is both an oxidizing and reducing agent.

# NOBEL PRIZE WINNERS — 1901-1992

| YEAR | PHYSICS | CHEMISTRY | PHYSIOLOGY OR MEDICINE |
|---|---|---|---|
| 1901 | *W.C. Röntgen (Germany) | J.H. Van't Hoff (Netherlands) | E.A. von Behring (Germany) |
| 1902 | *H.A. Lorentz (Netherlands) P. Zeeman (Netherlands) | E. Fischer (Germany) | R. Ross (Great Britain) |
| 1903 | *H.A. Becquerel (France) *P. Curie (France) *M.S. Curie (France) | S.A. Arrhenius (Sweden) | N.R. Finsen (Denmark) |
| 1904 | Lord Rayleigh (Great Britain) | W. Ramsay (Great Britain) | *I.P. Pavlov (Russia) |
| 1905 | P. Lenard (Germany) | A. v. Baeyer (Germany) | *R. Koch (Germany) |
| 1906 | J.J. Thomson (Great Britain) | *H. Moissan (France) | *C. Golgi (Italy) S. Ramon y Cajal (Spain) |
| 1907 | *A.A. Michelson (U.S.A.) | E. Buchner (Germany) | C.L.A. Laveran (France) |
| 1908 | G. Lippmann (France) | *E. Rutherford (Great Britain) | *P. Ehrlich (Germany) *E. Metchnikoff (Russia) |
| 1909 | *G. Marconi (Italy) F. Braun (Germany) | W. Ostwald (Germany) | T. Kocher (Switzerland) |
| 1910 | J.D. van der Waals (Netherlands) | O. Wallach (Germany) | A. Kossel (Germany) |
| 1911 | W. Wien (Germany) | *M.S. Curie (France) | A. Gullstrand (Sweden) |
| 1912 | G. Dalen (Sweden) | V. Grignard (France) P. Sabatier (France) | A. Carrel (U.S.A.) |
| 1913 | H. Kamerlingh Onnes (Neth.) | A. Werner (Switzerland) | C. Richet (France) |
| 1914 | M. von Laue (Germany) | T.W. Richards (U.S.A.) | R. Barany (Austria) |
| 1915 | W.H. Bragg (Great Britain) W.L. Bragg (Great Britain) | R. Willstätter (Germany) | No award |
| 1916 | No award | No award | No award |
| 1917 | C.G. Barkla (Great Britain) | No award | No award |
| 1918 | *M. Planck (Germany) | *F. Haber (Germany) | No award |
| 1919 | J. Stark (Germany) | No award | J. Bordet (Belgium) |
| 1920 | C.E. Guillaume (Switzerland) | *W. Nernst (Germany) | A. Krogh (Denmark) |
| 1921 | *A. Einstein (Germany) | F. Soddy (Great Britain) | No award |
| 1922 | *N. Bohr (Denmark) | F.W. Aston (Great Britain) | A.V. Hill (Great Britain) O. Meyerhof (Germany) |
| 1923 | *R.A. Millikan (U.S.A.) | F. Pregl (Austria) | *F.G. Banting (Canada) J.J.R. Macleod (Canada) |
| 1924 | K.M.G. Siegbahn (Sweden) | No award | W. Einthoven (Netherlands) |
| 1925 | *J. Franck (Germany) *G. Hertz (Germany) | R. Zsigmondy (Germany) | No award |
| 1926 | J. Perrin (France) | T. Svedberg (Sweden) | J. Fibiger (Denmark) |
| 1927 | *A.H. Compton (U.S.A.) *C.T.R. Wilson (Great Britain) | H. Wieland (Germany) | J. Wagner-Jauregg (Austria) |
| 1928 | O.W. Richardson (Great Britain) | A. Windaus (Germany) | *C.J.H. Nicolle (France) |
| 1929 | L.V. de Broglie (France) | A. Harden (Great Britain) H.A.S. von Euler-Chelpin (Sweden) | E. Eijkman (Netherlands) F.G. Hopkins (Great Britain) |
| 1930 | C.V. Raman (India) | *H. Fischer (Germany) | K. Landsteiner (Austria) |
| 1931 | No award | C. Bosch (Germany) F. Bergius (Germany) | O. Warburg (Germany) |
| 1932 | W. Heisenberg (Germany) | I. Langmuir (U.S.A.) | C. Sherrington (Great Britain) E.D. Adrian (Great Britain) |
| 1933 | E. Schrödinger (Austria) P.A.M. Dirac (Great Britain) | No award | *T.H. Morgan (U.S.A.) |
| 1934 | No award | *H.C. Urey (U.S.A.) | G.H. Whipple (U.S.A.) G.R. Minot (U.S.A.) W.P. Murphy (U.S.A.) |
| 1935 | J. Chadwick (Great Britain) | F. Joliot (France) *I. Joliot-Curie (France) | H. Spemann (Germany) |
| 1936 | V.F. Hess (Austria) C.D. Anderson (U.S.A.) | P.J.W. Debye (Netherlands) | *H.H. Dale (Great Britain) O. Loewi (Austria) |
| 1937 | C.J. Davisson (U.S.A.) *G.P. Thomson (Great Britain) | W.N. Haworth (Great Britain) P. Karrer (Switzerland) | A. Szent-Györgyi (Hungary) |
| 1938 | *E. Fermi (Italy) | R. Kuhn (Germany) | C. Heymans (Belgium) |
| 1939 | *E.O. Lawrence (U.S.A.) | A.F.J. Butenandt (Germany) L. Ruzicka (Switzerland) | *G. Domagk (Germany) |
| 1940, 1941, 1942—No awards were given | | | |
| 1943 | O. Stern (U.S.A.) | G. von Hevesy (Hungary) | H. Dam (Denmark) E.A. Doisy (U.S.A.) |
| 1944 | *I.I. Rabi (U.S.A.) | *O. Hahn (Germany) | E.J. Erlanger (U.S.A.) H.S. Gasser (U.S.A.) |
| 1945 | W. Pauli (Austria) | A.I. Virtanen (Finland) | *A. Fleming (Great Britain) *H.W. Florey (Great Britain) *E.B. Chain (Great Britain) |
| 1946 | P.W. Bridgman (U.S.A.) | J.B. Sumner (U.S.A.) W.M. Stanley (U.S.A.) J.H. Northrop (U.S.A.) | *H.J. Muller (U.S.A.) |
| 1947 | E.V. Appleton (Great Britain) | R. Robinson (Great Britain) | *C.F. Cori (U.S.A.) *G.T. Cori (U.S.A.) B.A. Houssay (Argentina) |
| 1948 | P.M.S. Blackett (Great Britain) | A. Tiselius (Sweden) | *P.H. Müller (Switzerland) |
| 1949 | H. Yukawa (Japan) | W.F. Giauque (U.S.A.) | W.R. Hess (Switzerland) A. Moniz (Portugal) |
| 1950 | C.F. Powell (Great Britain) | O. Diels (Germany) K. Alder (Germany) | P.S. Hench (U.S.A.) *E.C. Kendall (U.S.A.) T. Reichstein (Switzerland) |

*Asterisk means there is more about this person in the encyclopedia under his/her name or in the index (Vol. 20).

# NOBEL PRIZE WINNERS (CONTINUED)

| YEAR | PHYSICS | CHEMISTRY | PHYSIOLOGY OR MEDICINE |
|---|---|---|---|
| 1951 | J. Cockcroft (Great Britain)<br>*E.T. Walton (Great Britain) | E.M. McMillan (U.S.A.)<br>*G.T. Seaborg (U.S.A.) | M. Theiler (U.S.A.) |
| 1952 | E.M. Purcell (U.S.A.)<br>*F. Bloch (U.S.A.) | A.J.P. Martin (Great Britain)<br>R.L.M. Synge (Great Britain) | *S.A. Waksman (U.S.A.) |
| 1953 | F. Zernike (Netherlands) | H. Staudinger (Germany) | F.A. Lipmann (U.S.A.)<br>*H.A. Krebs (Great Britain) |
| 1954 | M. Born (Great Britain)<br>W. Bothe (Germany) | *L.C. Pauling (U.S.A.) | J.F. Enders (U.S.A.)<br>*T.H. Weller (U.S.A.)<br>F.C. Robbins (U.S.A.) |
| 1955 | W.E. Lomb, Jr. (U.S.A.)<br>P. Kusch (U.S.A.) | V. du Vigneaud (U.S.A.) | A.H. Theorell (Sweden) |
| 1956 | J. Bardeen (U.S.A.)<br>W. Brattain (U.S.A.)<br>W. Shockley (U.S.A.) | N. Semenov (U.S.S.R.)<br>*C. Hinshelwood (Great Britain) | A. Cournand (U.S.A.)<br>D.W. Richards, Jr. (U.S.A.)<br>W. Forssmann (West Germany) |
| 1957 | Chen Ning-Yang (U.S.A.)<br>Tsung Dao-Lee (U.S.A.) | A. Todd (Great Britain) | D. Bovet (Italy) |
| 1958 | P.A. Cherenkov (U.S.S.R.)<br>I.E. Tamm (U.S.S.R.)<br>I.M. Frank (U.S.S.R.) | F. Sanger (Great Britain) | J. Lederberg (U.S.A.)<br>G.W. Beadle (U.S.A.)<br>E.L. Tatum (U.S.A.) |
| 1959 | E. Segre (U.S.A.)<br>O. Chamberlain (U.S.A.) | J. Heyrovsky (Czechoslovakia) | *S. Ochoa (U.S.A.)<br>A. Kornberg (U.S.A.) |
| 1960 | D.A. Glaser (U.S.A.) | *W.F. Libby (U.S.A.) | *F.M. Burnet (Australia)<br>*P.B. Medawar (Great Britain) |
| 1961 | R. Hofstadter (U.S.A.)<br>*R. Mossbauer (U.S.A.) | M. Calvin (U.S.A.) | G. von Bekesy (U.S.A.) |
| 1962 | L.D. Landau (U.S.S.R.) | *M. Perutz (Great Britain)<br>J.C. Kendrew (Great Britain) | J.D. Watson (U.S.A.)<br>M.H.F. Wilkins (Great Britain)<br>F.H.C. Crick (Great Britain) |
| 1963 | E.P. Wigner (U.S.A.-Hungary)<br>M. Goeppert-Mayer (U.S.A.)<br>J.H. Jensen (Germany) | C. Zeigler (Germany)<br>G. Natta (Italy) | A.L. Hodgkin (Great Britain)<br>A.F. Huxley (Great Britain)<br>*J.C. Eccles (Australia) |
| 1964 | C.H. Townes (U.S.A.)<br>N.G. Basov (U.S.S.R.)<br>A.M. Prokhorov (U.S.S.R.) | D. Crowfoot Hogdkin (Great Britain) | K.E. Bloch (U.S.A.)<br>F.L. Lynen (Germany) |
| 1965 | R.P. Feynman (U.S.A.)<br>J.S. Schwinger (U.S.A.)<br>S. Tomonaga (Japan) | R.B. Woodward (U.S.A.) | F. Jacob (France)<br>A. Lwolff (France)<br>J. Monod (France) |
| 1966 | A. Kastler (France) | R. Sanderson Mulliken (U.S.A.) | C.B. Huggins (U.S.A.)<br>F.P. Rous (U.S.A.) |
| 1967 | H.A. Bethe (U.S.A.) | M. Eigen (West Germany)<br>R.G.W. Norrish (Great Britain)<br>G. Porter (Great Britain) | H.K. Hartline (U.S.A.)<br>G. Wald (U.S.A.)<br>R. Granit (Sweden) |
| 1968 | L.W. Alvarez (U.S.A.) | L. Ansager (U.S.A.) | R.W. Holley (U.S.A.)<br>H. Khorana (U.S.A.)<br>M.W. Nirenberg (U.S.A.) |
| 1969 | M. Gell-Mann (U.S.A.) | D.H.R. Barton (Great Britain)<br>O. Hassel (Norway) | M. Delbruck (U.S.A.)<br>S.E. Luria (U.S.A.)<br>A.D. Hershey (U.S.A.) |
| 1970 | *L. Neel (France)<br>H. Alfven (Sweden) | L.F. Leloir (France-Argentina) | J. Axelrod (U.S.A.)<br>B. Katz (Great Britain)<br>U. von Euler (Sweden) |
| 1971 | *D. Gabor (Great Britain) | *G. Herzberg (Canada) | E.W. Sutherland, Jr. (U.S.A.) |
| 1972 | J. Bardeen (U.S.A.)<br>*L. Cooper (U.S.A.)<br>*J.R. Schrieffer (U.S.A.) | C. Anfinsen (U.S.A.)<br>S. Moore (U.S.A.)<br>W.H. Stein (U.S.A.) | G.M. Edelman (U.S.A.)<br>*R.R. Porter (Great Britain) |
| 1973 | L. Esaki (Japan)<br>I. Giaever (U.S.A.)<br>B.D. Josephson (Great Britain) | *E.O. Fischer (Germany)<br>G. Wilkinson (Great Britain) | K. von Frisch (Austria)<br>*K.Z. Lorenz (Austria)<br>*N. Tinbergen (Netherlands) |
| 1974 | A. Hewish (Great Britain)<br>M. Ryle (Great Britain) | P.J. Flory (U.S.A.) | A. Claude (France)<br>C.R. de Duve (Belgium)<br>G.E. Palade (U.S.A.) |
| 1975 | J. Rainwater (U.S.A.)<br>A.N. Bohr (Denmark)<br>B.R. Mottelson (Denmark) | J.W. Cornforth (Great Britain)<br>*V. Prelog (Switzerland) | D. Baltimore (U.S.A.)<br>R. Dulbecco (U.S.A.)<br>H.M. Temin (U.S.A.) |
| 1976 | B. Richter (U.S.A.)<br>S.C.C. Ting (U.S.A.) | *W.N. Lipscomb, Jr. (U.S.A.) | B.S. Blumberg (U.S.A.)<br>*D.C. Gajdusek (U.S.A.) |
| 1977 | P.W. Anderson (U.S.A.)<br>J.H. Von Vleck (U.S.A.)<br>Sir N.F. Mott (U.S.A.) | I. Prigogine (Belgium) | R. Guillemin (U.S.A.)<br>A.V. Schally (U.S.A.)<br>R.S. Yalow (U.S.A.) |
| 1978 | P. Kapitsa (U.S.S.R.)<br>A. Penzias (U.S.A.)<br>R. Wilson (U.S.A.) | P. Mitchell (Great Britain) | W. Arber (Switzerland)<br>D. Nathans (U.S.A.)<br>H.O. Smith (U.S.A.) |
| 1979 | S.L. Glashow (U.S.A.)<br>S. Weinberg (U.S.A.)<br>A. Salam (Pakistan) | H.C. Brown (U.S.A.)<br>G. Wittig (Germany) | A.M. Cormack (U.S.A.)<br>G.N. Hounsfield (Great Britain) |
| 1980 | J.W. Cronin (U.S.A.)<br>V.L. Fitch (U.S.A.) | P. Berg (U.S.A.)<br>W. Gilbert (U.S.A.)<br>F. Sanger (Great Britain) | B. Benacerraf (U.S.A.)<br>G.D. Snell (U.S.A.)<br>J. Dausset (France) |
| 1981 | N. Bloembergen (U.S.A.)<br>A.L. Schawlow (U.S.A.)<br>K.M. Siegbahn (Sweden) | K. Fukui (Japan)<br>R. Hoffmann (U.S.A.) | R. Sperry (U.S.A.)<br>D. Hubel (U.S.A.)<br>T. Wiesel (U.S.A.) |
| 1982 | K.G. Wilson (U.S.A.) | A. Klug (Great Britain) | S. Bergstrom (Sweden)<br>B. Samuelsson (Sweden)<br>J.R. Vane (U.S.A.) |

| YEAR | PHYSICS | CHEMISTRY | PHYSIOLOGY OR MEDICINE |
|---|---|---|---|
| 1983 | S. Chandrasekhar (U.S.A.)<br>W.A. Fowler (U.S.A.) | H. Taube (Canada) | B. McClintock (U.S.A.) |
| 1984 | C. Rubbia (Italy)<br>S. van de Meer (Netherlands) | B. Merrifield (U.S.A.) | N.K. Jerne (Switzerland)<br>J.F. Kohler (Switzerland)<br>C. Milstein (Great Britain) |
| 1985 | K. von Klitzing (Germany) | H.A. Hauptmann (U.S.A.)<br>J. Karle (U.S.A.) | M.S. Brown (U.S.A.)<br>J.L. Goldstein (U.S.A.) |
| 1986 | E. Ruska (Germany)<br>G. Binnig (Germany)<br>H. Rohrer (Switzerland) | D. Herschbach (U.S.A.)<br>Y.T. Lee (U.S.A.)<br>J.C. Polanyi (Canada) | R. Levi-Montalcini (U.S.A.)<br>S. Cohen (U.S.A.) |
| 1987 | K.A. Muller (Switzerland)<br>G. Bednorz (Germany) | D.J. Cram (U.S.A.)<br>C.J. Pederson (U.S.A.)<br>J. Lehn (France) | S. Tonegawa (Japan) |
| 1988 | L.M. Lederman (U.S.A.)<br>M. Schwartz (U.S.A.)<br>J. Steinberger (U.S.A.) | J. Diesenhofer (Germany)<br>R. Huber (Germany)<br>H. Michel (Germany) | G.B. Elion (U.S.A.)<br>G.H. Hitchings (U.S.A.)<br>J. Black (Great Britain) |
| 1989 | N.F. Ramsey (U.S.A.)<br>H. Dehmelt (U.S.A.)<br>W. Paul (Germany) | S. Altman (U.S.A.)<br>T. Cech (U.S.A.) | J.M. Bishop (U.S.A.)<br>H.E. Varmus (U.S.A.) |
| 1990 | R. Taylor (Canada)<br>J.I. Friedman (U.S.A.)<br>H.W. Kendall (U.S.A.) | E.J. Corey (U.S.A.) | J.E. Murray (U.S.A.)<br>E.D. Thomas (U.S.A.) |
| 1991 | P. deGennes (France) | R.R. Ernst (Switzerland) | E. Neher (Germany)<br>B. Sakmann (Germany) |
| 1992 | G. Charpak (France) | R.A. Marcus (U.S.A.) | E.H. Fischer (U.S.A.)<br>E.G. Krebs (U.S.A.) |

**Nobel Prize** The Nobel Prizes are a group of awards given each year under the will of Alfred B. Nobel, a Swedish industrialist and the inventor of dynamite. According to the will, the prizes are to be awarded "to those who, during the *preceding year* had conferred the greatest benefit to mankind" in the fields of literature, world peace, physics, chemistry, and physiology or medicine.

The winners receive a portion of the income from Nobel's great fortune; the amount of the income varies each year. The recipients also receive gold medals. The Nobel Prizes are probably the most important international awards for human achievement.

Alfred Bernhard Nobel was born on October 21, 1833, in Stockholm, Sweden. He received most of his education from tutors. By the time Nobel was sixteen, he was a capable chemist and spoke five languages.

The prizes sprang from Nobel's own interests—his interest in ideas as expressed in literature; his interest in the effects of scientific achievement on health and medical knowledge; and his interest in chemistry and physics, as evidenced by his own career.

Nobel's fortune received its start when he devised a kind of NITROGLYCERIN that was less dangerous than the one formerly used. This work was followed by the invention of dynamite and by numerous other discoveries.

**Nobelium** (noh-BELL-ee-um) Nobelium is a man-made element first synthesized at the Nobel Institute in 1957.

In 1958 this element was confirmed by scientists in Berkley, California. It was formed by bombarding CURIUM, another man-made element, with nuclei of carbon atoms accelerated to nearly the speed of light by a cyclotron.

Nobelium (symbol No) is element number 102. The mass number of its most stable isotope is 255.          J.R.S.

SEE ALSO: ATOM, ELEMENTS

**Nocturnal habits** Many animals sleep during the day and hunt for their food at night. These are animals with nocturnal habits.

The hippopotamus feeds on grasses and reeds at night. Lions, tigers, and most other cat-family species hunt during the night for their prey. The coyote is noted for his night-time howl. Otter, weasel, ermine, American badger, raccoon and oppossum are all mainly night-active. Bats fly at night and capture insects at that time.

Many invertebrates are nocturnal. Earthworms crawl aboveground on cool, dewy summer evenings. There they feed on decaying plants; and, in proper season, mate at night aboveground.

The North American tarantula and the European earwig come out after dark to hunt.

Many desert animals are nocturnal because it is cooler after dark

The bear sometimes feeds at night

The skunk captures insects and small animals

Katydids, and some species of crickets, sing their familiar songs during the night. Most moths fly after sunset, when they gather nectar from night-blooming flowers. Among lower vertebrates, many kinds of frogs, lizards, and snakes are busy at night.

Among the flying vertebrates, the owl is the most well-known nocturnal BIRD OF PREY. In dim light it can see to swoop down on tiny rodents. Under similar light conditions, the whippoorwill scoops insects into its mouth while flying. Many water birds, especially herons, fish at night.

### NOCTURNAL ADAPTATION

The reasons animals are active at night vary with the species. In some species, special body structures account for an animal's nocturnal activities. An owl inherits large-pupiled eyes that enable it to see in dim light. Bats have echo-sensitive ears and wingtips; and as they fly, they emit ultrasonic squeaks, the reflection of which tell them what obstacles lie before them in the dark. Moles have super-sensitive touch and smell organs that enable the animal to work well in little light.

Most species of nocturnal animals have no observable body features which differ from those of day-active (*diurnal*) species, and are thought to be active at night because of in-born, instinctive ADAPTATIONS. For example, young pet mice remain most active at night even though their owner is active near them only during daytime.

The in-born night activity of such instinctually-adjusted animals is clearly useful in their survival; since they can avoid their day-prowling enemies and can, in turn, seek food or prey and move about more freely at night. They are free of competition with the diurnally active species living in their territory.

Two of the many reasons for instinctive night activity are *high temperature* and *intense light*. When bats are put into experimental caged rooms having low light and moderate temperature, they will fly about as if it were nighttime. When these bats are provided with artificial lights and higher tem-

perature, they will hang sleepily from the roosts. Studies of this type are part of experimental ECOLOGY.     M. R. L.

SEE ALSO: ANIMAL, BAT, BIRD, NIGHT-BLOOMING PLANTS

**Node** A node is the region of the STEM of a plant from which leaves and BUDS sprout. Spaces between nodes are called "internodes."

Underground stems may be distinguished from roots by the presence of nodes. Such plants as iris have underground stems called RHIZOMES. From the nodes of these rhizomes sprout the roots and leaves for new plants.     J. M. C.

**Noise** Noise is sound which is undesirable and unwanted because it has a bad effect such as interfering with speaking, reducing efficiency in work, damaging hearing, or masking a sound being listened for. Noises have irregular sound vibrations.

SEE ALSO: ACOUSTICS, DECIBELS, OVERTONES, SOUND

**Nonmetal** A nonmetal is one of a number of elements, including gases, liquids and solids, which are grouped together because they do not conduct heat or electricity well, are not ductile and malleable, and do not reflect light well. Chemically, nonmetal atoms form negative ions.

SEE: ELEMENTS, METAL

**Normality** Normality is a way of expressing the concentration of a solution. Normality is defined as the number of equivalents of *solute* per liter of *solvent*.

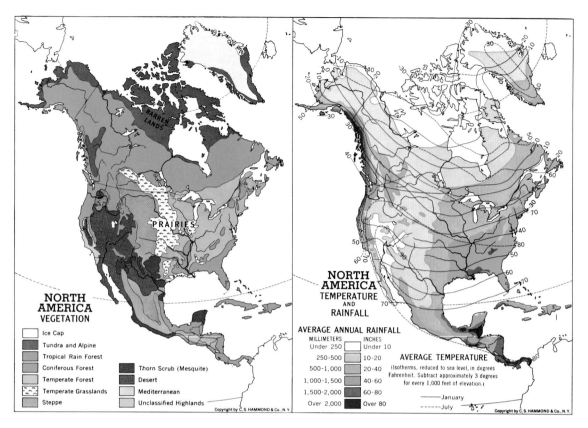

## LAND FORMS

**North America** North America is the third largest continent. It covers a sixth of the world's land—an area about 9,417,000 square miles (24,390,000 square kilometers). It is about 4,500 miles (7,242 kilometers) long and 4,000 miles (6,437 kilometers) wide. It is bounded on the north by the Arctic Ocean, on the east by the Atlantic Ocean, on the south by the Gulf of Mexico (part of the Atlantic) and South America, and on the west by the Pacific Ocean. The North American continent is divided into ten separate nations: Canada, United States, Mexico, Guatemala, Belize, Honduras, El Salvador, Nicaragua, Costa Rica, and Panama. There are also many island countries, such as Greenland, Cuba, Costa Rica, Dominican Republic, Hati, Jamaica, Bahamas, Barbados, and Trinidad.

The structure of North America shows that different parts of the continent have been subjected to different geologic forces over perhaps five billion years—the present estimate of the earth's age. From inside the earth great pressures have caused mountains to rise and erupt and valleys to form. From outside the earth water and winds have washed and swept over vast areas. The earth has undergone climatic changes (whose causes are not understood) from torrid heat to ice ages. Geologists are constantly trying to reconstruct the earth-forming time schedule, and they have been able, by surveying and digging and testing, to separate North America into five broad geologic parts.

The *Laurentian Upland*—or *Great Canadian Shield*—extends from Labrador in a semicircle around Hudson Bay, through the middle of the continent, as far south as the Lake Superior region, to the Arctic Ocean. The abundance of igneous and metamorphic rock, more than three billion years old, indicates that the area was once an ancient mountain range. The presence of marine deposits also indicates subsequent

# Map of
# NORTH AMERICA

SCALE OF MILES

0   200   400   600   800

✪ Capitals of Countries
• Cities
—·—·— Boundaries of Countries
▲ Mountain Peaks
====== Canals

Mountains  Highlands  Lowlands  Depression  Water

© Copyright HAMMOND INCORPORATED, Maplewood, N.J.

ASIA

ARCTIC OCEAN

North Pole

GREENLAND
(Danish)

ICELAND

Point Barrow

Bering Strait

Ellesmere Island

Thule

Baffin Bay

North Magnetic Pole

Victoria Island

Baffin Island

Davis Strait

UNITED STATES
Alaska
Yukon River

Anchorage

Juneau

Whitehorse

Mackenzie River

Great Bear Lake

Arctic Circle

Labrador

Hudson Bay

C A N A D A

Newfoundland

Queen Charlotte Islands

Great Slave Lake

Churchill

Goose Bay

St. Pierre & Miquelon (French)

Vancouver Island

Edmonton

Lake Winnipeg

St. Lawrence River

Halifax
Nova Scotia

40°

Seattle

Vancouver

Calgary

Winnipeg

Montréal
Ottawa

Toronto

Boston

Portland

Columbia

Great Lakes

Minneapolis

Detroit

Cleveland

New York

Philadelphia

Washington

San Francisco

Great Salt Lake

Salt Lake City

Missouri River

Chicago

APPALACHIAN MOUNTAINS

Cape Hatteras

Bermuda (British)

30°

Denver

Kansas City

St. Louis

Mt. Whitney

Colorado River

U N I T E D   S T A T E S

Memphis

Mt. Mitchell

Atlanta

Los Angeles

Phoenix

Dallas

New Orleans

Jacksonville

Cape Canaveral

San Diego

El Paso

Houston

Rio Grande

Mississippi River

B A H A M A S

Tropic of Cancer

Miami

Lower California

Monterrey

Gulf of Mexico

Havana

C U B A

HAITI

DOMINICAN REPUBLIC

PUERTO RICO (to U.S.)

Guadalajara

Mexico City

Veracruz

Yucatán Peninsula

JAMAICA

W e s t   I n d i e s

CARIBBEAN SEA

M E X I C O

BELIZE

HONDURAS

GUATEMALA

NICARAGUA

VENEZUELA

10°

EL SALVADOR

CENTRAL
AMERICA

COSTA RICA

PANAMA

CANAL ZONE (to U.S.)

Panama Canal

COLOMBIA

S O U T H

Equator

Galápagos Islands (Ecuadoran)

ECUADOR

A M E R I C A

BRAZIL

10°

BOLIVIA

PACIFIC OCEAN

ATLANTIC OCEAN

120°   110°   Longitude   100°   West of   90°   Greenwich   80°   70°

ROCKY MOUNTAINS

SIERRA NEVADA

SIERRA MADRE

Great Plains

submersion under a Paleozoic sea. The Canadian Shield region is also well known for the large number of *astroblemes* found there. Astroblemes are fossil meteorite impact craters. Only the deepest portions of these craters remain today, but are sufficient to remind us of the intense bombardment of the earth by meteorites since time began. The hardness of the rocks found here help preserve what remains to be seen. During Pleistocene times, four great ice sheets (the last receded only 10,000 years ago) spread out from this area on all sides, sweeping away rocks and soils, and scattering boulders and gravel as far south as southern Illinois.

The *Appalachian Area*—a hilly and mountainous belt stretching along the east coast from Newfoundland to Alabama, with a scattered part in Arkansas—was probably part of the original pre-Cambrian land mass. It has been subjected to repeated underground forces which caused the northern part to become an ARCHIPELAGO. The Appalachians have been worn down by EROSION and are full of fertile valley farm areas. Higher places are full of igneous and metamorphic rock. Worn slopes contain faulted and folded sedimentary rocks.

The *Coastal Plain* lies between the Appalachians and the sea, starting at Cape Cod and bordering the continent as far as Yucatan. The land is level and low with many sandy, marshy sections toward the south. The rocks are sedimentary.

The *Great Plains* extend from the Arctic to the Mississippi, from the Appalachians to the Rocky Moutains. This is the level and rolling mid-section of the continent, some of the best agricultural land in the world. Glaciers covered roughly one-half of the area, leaving soil-enriching pulverized limestone and sedimentary rock.

*Cordillera,* or *Western Highlands,* are the great system of mountain ranges that border the Pacific, sweeping from the northwestern tip of Alaska through Central America. Included are the Sierra Nevadas and Sierra Madres, the Coast Ranges, Cascade Range, and Rocky Mountains, all formed in recent geological time, about sixty-five million years ago. The region contains igneous, metamorphic, sedimentary, and recent volcanic rock. Torrential streams have carved great canyons. The terrain varies from the breathtaking heights of mountain peaks such as Mt. McKinley in Alaska, 20,300 feet (6,187 meters) and Mount Rainier in Washington, 14,140 feet (4,310 meters) to depths such as the Grand Canyon and Death Valley 280 feet (85 meters) below sea level).

## RIVERS AND DRAINAGE

Eight great North American river systems flowing toward the sea in all four directions have developed through successive crustal movements of the earth. The great Missouri-Mississippi system, emptying into the Gulf of Mexico, has an eastern branch, the Tennessee, Ohio and Illinois, and a western branch, the Red, Arkansas and Platte. The MacKenzie, flowing north into the Arctic, is fed by the Athabaska and Peace rivers. The Nelson flows northeast into Hudson Bay. The St. Lawrence flows northeast into the Atlantic. The Yukon in Alaska flows northwest into the Pacific. The Snake and Columbia flow west into the Pacific. The Colorado flows southwest into the Gulf of California, and the Rio Grande flows southeast into the Gulf of Mexico.

The five large Great Lakes—Superior, Michigan, Huron, with Niagara River and the Falls linking Erie and Ontario—are essentially part of the St. Lawrence drainage system. Other large fresh water lakes— Great Bear, Great Slave, Athabaska, and Winnipeg in Canada—are part of the MacKenzie or Nelson systems. These lakes are a result of glacier deposits and erosion. Great Salt Lake in Utah is a land-locked, shrinking remnant of a lake from the Pleistocene age. Much water has evaporated, leaving the heavier salts.

## CLIMATE

Most of North America is in the Temperate Zone of the Northern Hemisphere. The warm, moist ocean winds blow along both Atlantic and Pacific coasts with the result that relatively less temperature change occurs from winter to summer than inland. Warm winds from the Pacific are blocked by western mountain ranges so that in the winter the interior of the continent experiences a mean temperature of 0° F. (-17.8° C.) or less from Hudson Bay to the Central Northern United States. In summer, the great middle land area is warmer (mean temperature 65° to 80° F. or 18.3° to 26.7° C.) than the coastal areas.

1. **MOUNTAIN SHEEP**

Chicago Natural
History Museum

2. **MULE DEER**

Chicago Natural
History Museum

3. **BEAVER**

U.S. Forest Service

4. **LABRADOR DUCK**

Chicago Natural
History Museum

5. **PUMA**

Chicago Natural
History Museum

6. **MANATEE**

Chicago Natural
History Museum

7. **CHIPMUNK**

Courtesy Society For
Visual Education, Inc.

Rainfall, always caused by the cooling and condensation of moist air, is heaviest along the western slope of the Cordilleras where the ocean breezes are precipitated. Since the winds lose much of their moisture crossing the Rockies the central plains are relatively dry. The southwest area of the United States, in the lee of the mountains, is a low, dry, and arid desert land.

### PLANTS AND ANIMALS

The barren northern part of North America can grow only LICHEN, reindeer moss, and a few flowering plants during the short summer. The animal life of the north includes WALRUS, polar bear, caribou, fur seal, arctic fox, BEAVER, OTTER, and MARTEN.

Further south are found low shrubs and willows. Middle and southern Canada are covered with great forests of cone-bearing trees, SPRUCE, FIR, HEMLOCK, PINE. Here are found moose, deer, and black bear.

The Eastern Appalachians, to Gulf of Mexico, have HARDWOOD conifers, and birches, poplar, and maple in the north. There are OAK, HICKORY, and ELM in the middle area; WALNUT and TULIP TREES grow toward the south. The southern coastal plain has cypress and magnolias, mangroves, tropical palms, bamboos, rubber trees, silk-cotton, longwood, and mahogany forests.

The great plains grow a native sod grass but have few trees except for cottonwoods along the banks of rivers. The bison was native to this region but is now almost extinct. Giant REDWOOD forests, nurtured by heavy rains, prevail in the northwest and desert plants in the southwest.

The following animals are native to many western areas: puma (American lion), grizzly bear, gopher, muskrat, prairie dog, beaver, porcupine, raccoon, skunk, musk ox, big horn (Rocky Mountain sheep), pronghorn (antelope), rocky mountain goat, and opossum.

Native birds include the Baltimore oriole, bobolink, cowbird, flycatcher, wild turkey, and wood warblers. There are only four poisonous snakes: rattler, copperhead, cottonmouth, and coral. Alligators are found near the Gulf of Mexico.

### NATURAL RESOURCES

Natural resources mean what mankind can turn into wealth, either to improve the material culture or to provide non-material wealth like recreation. North America is rich in resources, both in what can be grown above the ground, and what can be extracted out of the ground. It has the climate and soil to grow every type of crop. The principal ones are wheat, oats, corn, barley, sugar, apples, grapefruit, oranges, and tobacco. The structure of North America has been shown to be varied. Certain regions, where igneous and metamorphic rock abound, contain metals. In other regions, characterized by sedimentary rock, valuable nonmetallic materials are likely to be found. Copper, gold, iron, silver, nickel and many other metals are mined extensively in North America. Chemicals such as salts and phosphates, building materials of stone and clay, ceramic materials, and gem-stones are all dug out of the earth and utilized by man. Mineral fuels such as coal, oil and gas are other vital natural resources that are plentiful in North America. H. W. M.
SEE ALSO: CONTINENT, EARTH, GEOLOGIC TIME TABLE, NATURAL RESOURCES, ROCKS

**North Atlantic drift** After the Gulf Stream curves out to the east off the GRAND BANKS of Newfoundland, it widens and slows down. Here it is called the *North Atlantic drift*. It crosses the Atlantic and sends off numerous branches of warmer water into the Arctic.

According to recent theory the warmer waters of the North Atlantic drift cause heavy snows which build the mighty polar ice cap. After centuries of accumulating polar ice, the sea level drops so that the currents can no longer penetrate the Arctic. The snows stop and the cap slowly melts, and thus the sea returns to its former level. The cycle is then repeated. R. N. J.
SEE ALSO: CURRENTS, OCEAN; GULF STREAM

**North pole** see Magnet; Poles, North and South

**North Star** see Polaris, Ursa Major and Ursa Minor

**Northern Cross** see Cygnus

**Northern lights** see Aurora Borealis

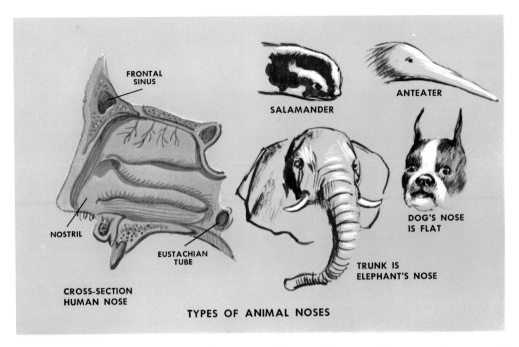

FRONTAL SINUS

SALAMANDER

ANTEATER

NOSTRIL

EUSTACHIAN TUBE

DOG'S NOSE IS FLAT

TRUNK IS ELEPHANT'S NOSE

CROSS-SECTION HUMAN NOSE

**TYPES OF ANIMAL NOSES**

**Nose** The nose is an area on the front end of the head. It usually has two openings. Some animal noses stick out as man's does. The trunk of an elephant is its nose. Most animals, however, have flat noses which are part of the upper jaw area. The nose is used to smell things that are in air or water. Animals with lungs use the nose in breathing.

The external nose is made of skin, bone, and CARTILAGE. The internal nose consists of two airways separated by a *septum*. The minute hairs in the nose function as air filters. The cells lining the tubes secrete mucus which moistens the surface. The olfactory nerves are stimulated when certain odors reach the nose. These chemo-receptors send the message to the brain.      H. J. C.

SEE ALSO: RESPIRATORY SYSTEM

**Notochord** A notochord (or *notocord*) is a rod of hard tissue found in the young of all chordates and some adult lower chordates. It lies between the central NERVOUS SYSTEM and digestive tract. The vertebrae form around it.

SEE: CHORDATA, EMBRYOLOGY

**Nova** (NOH-vah) A nova is a very dim star that suddenly flares up and becomes very bright. It stays bright for a short period of time and then gradually fades back to its former faintness.

More than 100 typical novae have been seen in the Milky Way galaxy and more are discovered each year. Astronomers have estimated that about 25 novae appear yearly in the Milky Way. At least five typical novae became stars of the first MAGNITUDE, or brighter than the first magnitude, in this century.

Typical novae are subdwarf stars that are much smaller than our sun. The most characteristic thing about novae is the variation of light that they radiate. This ranges from a single, abrupt rise to maximum brightness to a very slow fading. Often the fading is interrupted by short and partial recovery of brightness. The rise in brightness, at its peak, may be more than 12 magnitudes, an increase in brightness of more than 60,000 times.    H. S. G.

SEE ALSO: NEBULA; STAR; STAR, VARIABLE

**Novocaine** (NOH-vuh-cane) Novocaine is a very complex salt, injected in solution as a local ANESTHETIC in minor surgery and dentistry. It is a nontoxic substitute for cocaine.

## Nuclear energy

**Nuclear energy** Nuclear energy is the energy made available when a nucleus (except hydrogen) is formed (FUSION) or broken up (FISSION). When only small pieces of the nucleus fly off or when electromagnetic radiation is given off, these disintegrations are called *radioactive decay*.

Nuclear energy is *not* atomic energy. Atomic energy deals with changes in the atom outside of the nucleus. Nuclear energy concerns the energy and particles inside the nucleus and the energy of elementary particles.

Today's NUCLEAR REACTORS—fission reactors—allow us to explore radioactive decay in depth. They also permit us to bombard ordinary nuclei in normal atoms to make them radioactive. Use of these man-made or human-controlled radioactive sources may lead to fantastic changes in our lives. Irradiated meat, for example, can be kept at room temperature for months without spoiling. The use of radioactive tracers in medicine yields sharp photographs of soft tissues, something once considered impossi-

General Dynamics photo

Nuclear energy is gaining wide use in nuclear-powered submarines. They are driven by energy from a nuclear reactor and can stay submerged for many weeks

ble. RADIATION is even being used to sterilize processed sewage sludge; in experimental trials, these mineral-rich wastes have been used as a dietary supplement for livestock.

The explosive power released in nuclear reactions has also been harnessed for military purposes. Both fission and fusion weapons have been developed and tested. There has even been discussion of using nuclear

**SLOW NEUTRONS HIT URANIUM-235 ATOMS TO START A *FISSION* CHAIN REACTION; PRODUCTS CAN VARY**

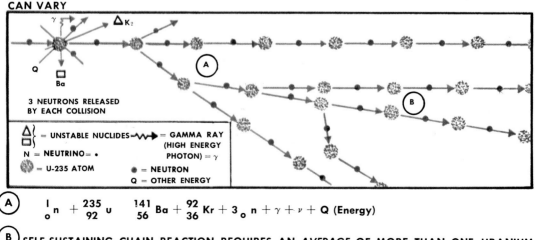

$$\text{A} \quad {}_{0}^{1}n + {}_{92}^{235}U \quad {}_{56}^{141}Ba + {}_{36}^{92}Kr + 3\,{}_{0}n + \gamma + \nu + Q \text{ (Energy)}$$

**B** SELF-SUSTAINING CHAIN REACTION REQUIRES AN *AVERAGE* OF MORE THAN ONE URANIUM ATOM-NEUTRON COLLISION FOR EACH FISSION OF A URANIUM ATOM

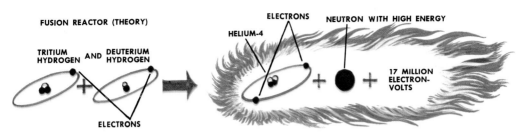

FUSION REACTOR (THEORY)

TRITIUM HYDROGEN **AND** DEUTERIUM HYDROGEN

ELECTRONS

ELECTRONS

HELIUM-4

NEUTRON WITH HIGH ENERGY

17 MILLION ELECTRON-VOLTS

**The energy of nuclear fusion cannot yet be controlled. So far it is useful only in nuclear explosions**

explosions for peaceful activities; for example, underground nuclear explosions could release trapped oil or natural-gas deposits.

### NUCLEAR FISSION

*Fission* reactions are those that cause the *splitting* of a heavy element's nucleus into two large fragments, plus two or more *neutrons* and RADIANT ENERGY. This fission process powers nuclear power plants throughout the world today—including those that are used aboard submarines and aircraft carriers.

The rate at which fission occurs can be controlled to provide a steady liberation of heat energy. Nuclear reactors, devices that control the rate of fissioning in uranium or plutonium fuel, use the heat of fission to create steam. That steam, in turn, drives turbines to create electricity.

As an energy source, nuclear fuel is very efficient. By weight, nuclear fuel produces about 2½ million times as much energy as would be created from the chemical burning of fossil fuels. In other words, one ton (.9 metric ton) of uranium can produce as much energy as 2½ million tons (2.25 million metric tons) of coal.

Although most nuclear reactors are used to heat steam for generating electric power, reactors do have other functions. Some are used to explore NUCLEAR SCIENCE and the way nuclear *chain reactions* may be controlled. Others are used to create radioactive elements that are used in medicine for the diagnosis and treatment of disease. Some are even used as teaching tools for training students of nuclear engineering.

### NUCLEAR FUSION

*Fusion* is a second type of nucleaꞁ that liberates enormous amounts of energy. It involves *joining,* or fusing, the nuclei of two light atoms. When this occurs, the total mass of the fused atom will be less than the combined mass of the initial, smaller atoms. The "lost" mass has actually been converted into energy in accordance with Einstein's famous equation: $E = mc^2$ (see MASS AND ENERGY).

Fusion is the process that powers the sun and stars. It is expected that when fusion power becomes commercially available on earth, *deuterium and tritium*—two heavy forms, of hydrogen called *isotopes*—will be the primary fuels. These isotopes are plentiful. A single gallon of ordinary water contains deuterium with an energy value equal to 300 gallons (1,136 liters) of gasoline. Therefore, if one turned to the oceans for this fusion fuel, there would be enough deuterium to fuel fusion reactors for a billion or more years. Tritium is formed by bombarding the prevalent element lithium with neutrons from fusion reactions.

There are two primary fusion reactions likely to be used for commercial power production. D-D reactions would fuse two deuterium nuclei. D-T reactions would fuse tritium and deuterium nuclei. Both the D-D and D-T reactions can produce nonradioactive helium nuclei. Alternatively, some D-D reactions will instead yield tritium and a *proton* (a hydrogen nucleus).

There have been two major approaches to developing commercial fusion-power plants: *magnetic confinement* and *inertial confinement*. To date, two major obstacles have limited the commercial harnessing of magnetic-confinement fusion power on earth. The first has been the heating of fuel to a high enough temperature—generally greater than 100 million degrees Celsius (180 million degrees Fahrenheit). At these temperatures, electrons tend to dissociate themselves from their nuclei. The resulting mixture of free nuclei and free electrons is termed an *ionized plasma*. The second obstacle has been determining how to hold the

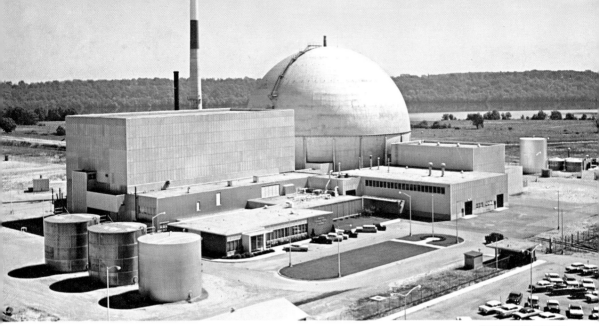

The Dresden-1 reactor near Chicago was the first American nuclear-power plant operated without government help. Completed in 1960, it shut down in 1978.

millions-of-degrees-hot plasma. Since the plasma has to be confined for its ionized nuclei to collide—and fuse—physicists have envisioned designing various *"magnetic bottles."* These are not true bottles; they are intense magnetic fields that serve as melt-proof walls to confine a plasma. A leading contender in the contest to develop the best magnetic bottle is the *tokamak.* Its magnetic coils provide a donut-shaped "bottle."

On December 24, 1982, the Tokamak Fusion Test Reactor of Princeton University confined its first plasma. It is expected that this device will be the first magnetic-confinement fusion machine to achieve ignition, or *scientific breakeven*—the condition of achieving as much energy from fusions as it took to confine and heat the plasma.

In inertial-confinement fusion, miniature pellets of deuterium and tritium fuel, approximately 1 millimeter (.04 inch) in diameter, are bombarded by intense laser beams or ion beams from many directions simultaneously. The goal is to make the pellets *implode* (explode inward). This action would both heat the fuel—to roughly 50 million degrees Celsius (90 million degrees Fahrenheit)—and compress the fuel dramatically for a few *nanoseconds* (billionths of a second). When both conditions are achieved—heating and adequate compression—the fuel may fuse. In a commercial inertia-confinement fusion device, the energy liberated by imploding between 10 and 50 pellets per second would heat water to drive turbines, generating electricity.

## MASS AND ENERGY

An atomic nucleus has less *mass* (closely related to weight) than the parts of the nucleus would have if they were separated and outside the nucleus. This difference, known as the *mass defect,* represents an amount of matter that changed into energy when the protons and neutrons came together to form the nucleus originally. This energy is called the *binding energy* of the nucleus. The greater the binding energy of the nucleus, the more stable that nucleus is, and therefore more energy is required to break it apart.

The binding energy of each kind of nucleus can be calculated. Such calculations show that the nuclei of elements from the middle of the *periodic table* (where chemical elements are arranged in order of increasing mass) are bound most firmly together. Those at either end of the periodic table can be broken apart with less energy. This leads to the possibility that energy can be liberated by changing either light nuclei or heavy nuclei into those of intermediate mass.

Scientists now believe that mass and energy are different indications of a fundamental fact of nature. Mass and energy are related mathematically as shown by the now-famous equation $E = mc^2$, which was stated first by the theoretical physicist ALBERT EINSTEIN in 1905. This equation states that if a quantity of matter, moving *mass,* m, is converted into energy, the amount of that energy is equal to the mass multiplied by the square of the velocity of light. All nuclear processes that liberate energy involve the transformation of one nucleus into one or more others. Although protons and neutrons are not destroyed, there is a decrease in the total mass.                    R.C.S.

SEE ALSO: BOMBS, NUCLEAR PARTICLES, NUCLEAR REACTORS, NUCLEAR SCIENCE, NUCLEAR SCIENCE GLOSSARY, RADIATION

**Nuclear particles** *Elementary particles,* as nuclear particles are now called, are supposedly the building blocks of the universe; from them, all MATTER and RADIATION are believed to have been formed.

The nearly 200 elementary particles that have been named are usually divided into several families, depending upon how they act. All are very small, about one thousandth of a trillionth centimeter in diameter. Although none have ever been viewed directly, scientists have been able to detect their presence by the tracks they leave behind; one might imagine them as being similar to tracks left behind by rabbits bounding through fresh snow. Particle tracks, however, are miniscule in size, and are detectable only by sensitive scientific monitors. In much the way a nature scout identifies an animal by the size and shape of its tracks, physicists study the curvature of tracks, together with information about several other important factors, such as energy, to identify particles.

New particles are found by accelerating PROTONS, NEUTRONS and other particles to extremely high energies and then hurling the particles at solid targets or other moving particles to split nuclei. The *Cockcroft-Walton* machine, *Van de Graaff generator, cyclotron, betatron,* and *synchro-cyclotron linear accelerator* are common particle-accelerating devices. For detecting their smashing results, photographs replace direct viewing. Among the frequently used detectors are the *ionization chamber, spark chamber, bubble chamber,* and *cloud chamber.*

Stalking new particles can even take on the drama and tension of a big-game hunt. Consider the recent search for two *intermediate vector bosons*—usually designated by the letters $W^+$ and $W^-$. In the 1930s, a Japanese physicist explained mathematically why intermediate particles might explain the four forces witnessed in nature: *gravity,*

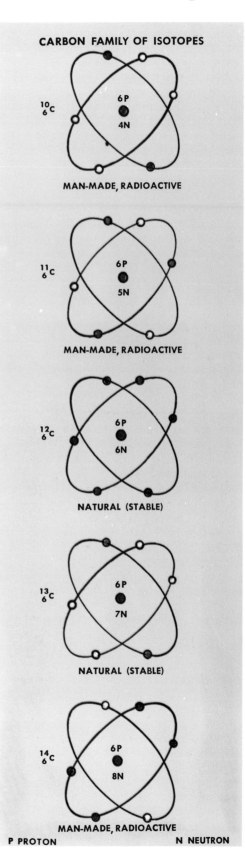

CARBON FAMILY OF ISOTOPES

$^{10}_{6}$C          6P 4N          MAN-MADE, RADIOACTIVE

$^{11}_{6}$C          6P 5N          MAN-MADE, RADIOACTIVE

$^{12}_{6}$C          6P 6N          NATURAL (STABLE)

$^{13}_{6}$C          6P 7N          NATURAL (STABLE)

$^{14}_{6}$C          6P 8N          MAN-MADE, RADIOACTIVE

P PROTON          N NEUTRON

*electromagnetism, weak interaction,* and *strong interaction.* Early in the 1970s, Steven Weinberg, Abdus Salam, and Sheldon Glashow developed mathematical equations suggesting that physicists might hunt for a new family of particles that would include two W particles and a Z particle. These particles would help explain the existence and operation of weak forces in nature. The three scientists shared a Nobel Prize for their theory.

Finding the particles, however, was left to a team of 120 physicists from 11 institutions in Europe and the United States. Together they collaborated on an experiment using a new and unconventional particle accelerator—a *proton-antiproton collider* at the European international physics laboratory called CERN in Geneva, Switzerland. In an experiment lasting 30 days, protons and antiprotons were hurled in opposite directions through a circular pipe. At several points in the ring, the particles were brought into head-on collisions. Though many tracks were recorded over the month of tests, only four strongly suggested the presence of W particles—exactly the number that would have been expected to appear. The scientists announced their discovery in January 1983, more than 10 years after Weinberg, Salam, and Glashow first suggested that the particles might exist.

Elementary particles can be classified into *hadrons* (which interact by "strong interactions"), *leptons* (which interact by "weak interactions"), the *photon,* and the *electromagnetic-interaction particle* (which exists in a class by itself).

Hadrons are further divided into *baryons* and *mesons.* In any interaction, the number of baryons must remain constant, although the type of baryon need not remain the same. Among the family of baryons are *hyperons* and *nucleons.* Hyperons—known to physicists as *strange particles*—all have masses greater than nucleons. Nucleons, which include the proton and neutron, have rest masses ranging from 1,836 to 6,000 times that of the tiny electron. Mesons also include strange particles (such as the *kaon*) and nonstrange particles (such as *pions*).

Leptons include the *muon* electron and two types of *neutrinos.* In any interaction, the number of leptons is also conserved. The massless *bosons*—which include the photon and graviton—have neither a rest mass nor charge, although both have a *spin* and energy.

With only two exceptions, each particle has an *antiparticle.* A particle and its antiparticle annihilate each other upon contact. Whenever a particle has an electric charge, its antiparticle will carry an electric charge of the opposite site sign. Two particles—the uncharged pion and the photon—serve as their own antiparticles.

In 1963, two scientists working separately suggested that all previously known or suspected particles might be made from unusual subparticles, which have come to be known as QUARKS. According to Murray Gell-Mann and George Zweig, these quarks would be the most basic integral particles in the universe.

Existing in sets of three, two of the quarks would have electric charges of $-\frac{1}{3}$ unit each; the third would have a charge of $+\frac{2}{3}$. Although quarks are still only theory—which means they have not yet been detected physically—scientists are coming more and more to suspect they are probably real. Research suggests there may be as many as six different types of quarks—a pair each of charmed quarks, strange quarks, up quarks, down quarks, bottom quarks, and top quarks. The unusual names physicists have given these suspected particles does not mean the subparticles themselves would actually be strange, charmed, above, or below others. These names are just physicists' clever nicknames for identifying the differentiating mathematical characteristics each quark would have.

All particles, quarks or larger, obey some or all of the 12 physical conservation laws, including conservation of energy, of momentum, of charge, of electron-family number, and of spin.                    M.S.P.

SEE ALSO: ELEMENTS, ISOTOPE, NUCLEAR SCIENCE, NUCLEAR SCIENCE GLOSSARY, RADIOACTIVITY

**Nuclear reactor** A nuclear reactor is a device for controlling nuclear reactions. The first nuclear reactor (then called an atomic pile) began to operate on December 2, 1942, at the University of Chicago. It was a result of knowledge accumulated by many scientists working over many years in several countries of the world. This first reactor was designed, built, and tested by a team of scientists under the leadership of the Italian Nobel Prize

The world's first nuclear reactor, CP-1, was built under the football stands of Stagg Field at the University of Chicago. An artist's drawing shows a number of famous physicists (upper left), including Enrico Fermi, among the spectators. Physicist George Weil is shown slowly pulling a cadmium control rod out of the reactor core, initiating a nuclear chain reaction.

winner, DR. ENRICO FERMI, who had left Italy in 1938.

Today, only *fission* reactors operate to produce commercial energy and *radioisotopes*. There are a multitude of different types of fission reactors, however. Among them are the *heavy-water reactors* (used primarily in Canada), *light-water-cooled reactors* (the most common type in operation around the world), *high-temperature gas-cooled reactors, light-water breeder reactors, liquid-metal fast breeder reactors,* and several other more experimental concepts.

A reactor must be designed in such a way that the desired actions will occur and all other possible happenings will be reduced adequately. In practice, this is very difficult. The quantity, purity, and arrangement of the fissionable fuels are of major importance. The energy, or velocity, of the neutrons must be controlled by the use of materials known as *moderators*. GRAPHITE is a practical material for this purpose. In many reactors, ordinary water and heavy water are sometimes used with the graphite or with BERYLLIUM or compounds of beryllium. The reactor must be provided with equipment for controlling the rate of the fission process. The entire assembly must be surrounded with materials that will protect nearby workers and shield them from harmful radiation.

## REACTOR FUEL

The only fuels used to power fission reactors are URANIUM-233, uranium-235, and PLUTONIUM-239. Uranium-235 occurs naturally and is mined in a manner similar to coal mining. Uranium-233 is created in reactors from thorium-232, a slightly radioactive element. (When a fission neutron is absorbed by thorium-232, thorium 233 is formed. That ISOTOPE decays in a several-step process to uranium-233.) Plutonium is also a fuel manufactured by fission in reactors. (When uranium-238 absorbs a fission neutron, uranium-239 results. This isotope decays naturally, in a several-step process, to plutonium-239.) Once produced, uranium-233 and plutonium-239 can be separated from

Argonne National Laboratory's Zero Gradient Synchrotron (ZGS) complex. This 12.5 giga-electron-volt proton accelerator was once a powerful source of polarized protons for particle research. ZGS was shut down in October 1979.

"used," or *spent reactor fuel,* through a process called *nuclear-fuel reprocessing.* Reprocessing upgrades the uranium-233 or plutonium-239 to fuel-grade purity so that it may be recycled to fuel other reactors.

To start and keep a reactor's fuel fissioning, a *critical mass* of atoms is required. When nuclei fission—that is, split—they release energy (RADIATION), nuclear fragments (often small atoms), and nuclear particles (which will include at least two neutrons). If the fuel is packed densely enough and in sufficient quantity to create a critical mass, then neutrons expelled during a fission reaction will be absorbed by the nuclei of other fissionable atoms (fuel). This will cause many of those nuclei to split—each ejecting two or more neutrons in the process. Because each neutron is capable of causing another fission, a *chain reaction* may be set up, whereby a single fission sets up a self-sustaining series of continuing fissions.

Human operators control the rate of fission in a reactor by controlling the *neutron flux,* or neutron intensity, which develops in its core area. If the neutron flux gets too high—inducing too many fissions and producing too much heat—then neutron-absorbing control rods are lowered into the reactor. If there are too few fissions per second, control rods are raised out of the reactor's central core to increase the

A rendering of the Cockcroft-Walton generator. It was used as the first stage of the Zero Gradient Synchrotron. This huge 12½ billion-electron-volt atom smasher has been used to study the fundamental building blocks of matter.

neutron flux. To shut down a reactor completely, all of the neutron-quenching control rods are dropped into the core area—simultaneously if necessary. To start up the reactor again, control rods can be slowly and selectively raised from the core, one by one.

In conventional nuclear reactors, the main function of the neutrons produced is to sustain an ongoing chain reaction. The larger fission fragments have another function: they produce heat. As fission frag-

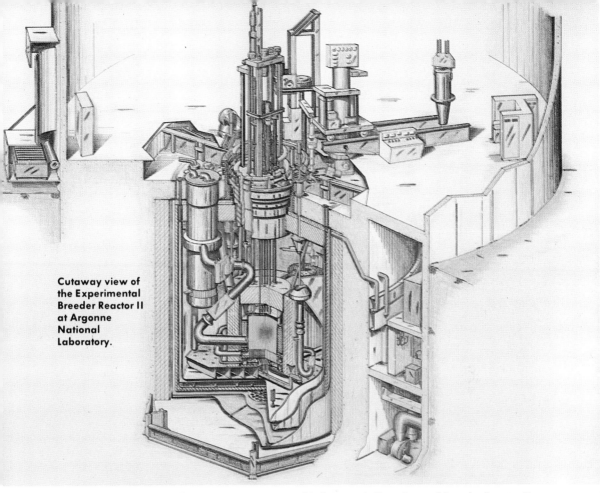

Cutaway view of the Experimental Breeder Reactor II at Argonne National Laboratory.

The reactor operating floor at Argonne National Laboratory's Experimental Breeder Reactor II. The column slightly right of center contains the control rod actuating control devices and some of the equipment necessary to handle reactor fuel. The reactor is contained in a large tank of molten sodium located beneath the floor plates. The equipment at left is used to remove radioactive fuel from the reactor.

Argonne National Laboratories

A top view of Experimental Breeder Reactor II before the tank surrounding it was filled with molten sodium. The mechanism in the foreground is lowering the last sub-assembly into the core. The rods in the center, are control rod drives. During operation these mechanisms are operated remotely, with the entire reactor submerged in molten sodium coolant.

ments collide with the nuclei of surrounding atoms, some of their *kinetic energy* is converted into *heat energy*. It is heat that actually generates power.

Almost 90 percent of the total energy produced in a nuclear reactor occurs as heat within the fissioning fuel. Another 5 percent of the energy—contributed by gamma radiation and fast-neutron energy—is converted to heat in the reactor *moderator* (a neutron-slowing substance), in the reactor-core *coolant* (usually some form of water), and in the reactor's structural materials.

The reactor-core coolant carries away heat generated in the core by fission, and transfers that heat to boil water, eventually creating steam. The steam then passes through a turbine generator to create electricity. From the steam stage on, a coal-fired power plant and nuclear power plant may be identical; the difference between them is in how they make steam.

## GROWTH OF NUCLEAR POWER

Commercial nuclear power was born at 12:39 AM, December 18, 1957. At that precise moment, Duquesne Light Co. engineers synchronized the turbine genera-

tor of a power plant in Shippingport, Pa., with the utility company's electricity-distribution network. By 7 AM the Shippingport Atomic Power Station was generating 12,000 kilowatts to homes and factories throughout the Pittsburgh area. By Christmas, the reactor had attained full power (68,000 kilowatts).

Small by today's standards, the experimental powerplant (operated jointly by Duquesne Light Co. and the federal government) produced 7.3 billion kilowatt-hours of electricity while testing several major commercial reactor concepts—including the light-water reactor and light-water-breeder reactor. Ironically, the Shippingport station was shut down on October 1, 1982, just two and a half months short of its 25th birthday.

Although Shippingport was the first commercial reactor—the first to produce power for paying customers—research reactors had preceded it. In fact, the world's first reactor was CP-1 at the University of Chicago. This small device, which single-handedly ushered in the nuclear age, "went critical"—that is, it sustained a controlled fission chain reaction—on December 2, 1942.

The Argonaut test reactor, shut down in 1972, was used in teaching and research.

By the time Shippingport shut down 40 years later, there were 82 nuclear reactors licensed to operate in the United States; together these plants generated roughly 10 percent of the nation's electric power. Outside the United States, there were 199 operable reactors and another 151 reactors under construction. France had the most aggressive nuclear-reactors development program. By 1981, 38 percent of the electricity in France came from nuclear power—the highest percentage anywhere in the world. By the mid-1980s, 22 countries had operating reactors and another 18 had reactors under construction or in the planning.

## NUCLEAR SAFETY

Nuclear power's once mushrooming growth began to slow in the mid-1970s as the cost of building reactors escalated dramatically. At this time, too, critics of nuclear power began questioning the safety of reactor designs. They also began questioning whether a way would be found to safely bury radioactive wastes—safeguarding them from the environment for the thousands of years the wastes would remain hazardous. Finally, with discussion of recycling used reactor fuel in the United States, critics began to question whether terrorists might be able to steal plutonium.

Plutonium is a radioactive fuel created in the fissioning core of uranium-fueled reactors. It is separated from "used fuel" during the fuel-recycling process. Although it makes an excellent fuel for *breeder reactors* (reactors that create more fuel than they consume), plutonium is also the material from which terrorists could most easily and safety fashion a crude nuclear weapon.

Eventually, reactor safety became the most widely debated issue of the continued growth of nuclear power in the United States, Europe, and Japan. The March 28, 1979, crippling of the Three Mile Island (Pa.) reactor and the catastrophic explosion in a nuclear reactor at Chernobyl, Soviet Union, in 1986 pointed out many general problems in the regulation, management, and design of commercial nuclear-powered plants. The Chernobyl accident released radiation and contaminated a wide area.

Since these nuclear accidents, every reactor in the United States has been altered to upgrade safety procedures and systems. Reactor operators now undergo far more intensive training. Government regulators have increased their monitoring and enforcement of safety rules at these plants. Reactor owners have also begun emergency planning; by law they must work out with the state and federal governments plans for protecting or evacuating local citizens in the event of a catastrophic reactor accident. The goal is to make reactors able to safely withstand accidents more severe than the one that damaged the Three Mile Island plant and to protect the public and the environment.

D.A.B.

SEE ALSO: NUCLEAR ENERGY, NUCLEAR PARTICLES, NUCLEAR SCIENCE, RADIATION

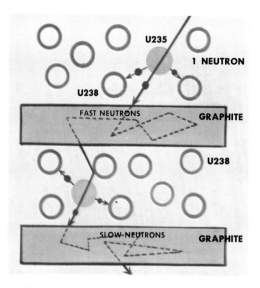

Natural uranium is a mixture of U-235 and U-238. U-235 can absorb either fast or slow neutrons. U-238 can absorb only slow neutrons. In the fission of U-235, fast neutrons are given off. These are slowed down by the graphite and thus, because of their slow speed, can be absorbed only by the U-235, creating a controlled chain reaction

**Nuclear science** Nuclear science has become the study of natural and man-made nuclear reactions. Through the investigation of nuclear interactions, physicists and engineers are acquiring a better understanding of *elementary particles* and various established principles of physics, including the *invariance principles* and the *law of conservation of energy.*

People in this field have three major goals. First, scientists seek constantly to find new knowledge. In nuclear science they want to know about the nature and behavior of the smallest particles of matter. Other workers, chiefly engineers, use this knowledge to develop and expand the production and uses of nuclear power. A third goal is the production of new *isotopes* that do not exist naturally on earth.

The investigation for new isotopes even extends to a search for and creation of entirely new elements. Some of the elements may prove useful: others will remain purely curiosities. Element 109, first created August 29 in Darmstadt, West Germany, lasted only a fraction of a second before decaying into element 104, which ultimately fissioned. It is expected such difficult-to-produce and extremely short-lived elements will never prove more than laboratory oddities.

### MATTER AND ENERGY

MATTER and ENERGY are very important in nuclear science. Both are involved in the behavior and use of atomic nuclei. Matter is defined as anything that has mass and occupies space. Everything that can be seen and handled is matter. Energy is usually invisible and therefore seems more difficult to understand. But the results of energy are seen in motion, as when the wind blows. Energy can also be felt in the form of heat.

### ATOMIC STRUCTURE

It is helpful, though not quite accurate, to compare the parts of the atom with a PLANET and its moons. One might think of an atom's nucleus as being a planet. Around it orbits electrons, much like miniature natural satellites.

Each ATOM of any particular chemical element will have the same number of protons in its nucleus. Nuclei with a single PROTON are HYDROGEN nuclei. Atoms whose nuclei contain six protons are CARBON. The most complex of all natural nuclei, those of the element URANIUM, contain 92 protons. The number of protons is called an element's *atomic number.*

Two atoms having the same atomic number may have different numbers of neutrons in their nuclei. If so, they are considered different ISOTOPES of the same element. The number of protons plus the number of neutrons is known as the *mass number.* The mass number of uranium-233 is 233. Uranium-233 and uranium-235 are different isotopes of the same element.

The nucleus of an atom is the part from which nuclear energy is liberated. Nuclear scientists usually focus their attentions on radioactive isotopes because their unstable nature makes these isotopes easy to transform from one element into another.

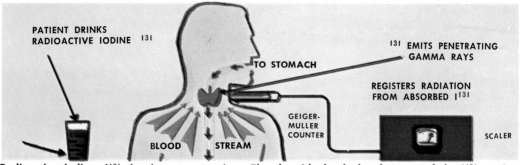

Radioactive iodine, I¹³¹, is given to a patient. The thyroid gland absorbs most of the I¹³¹ retained by the body. A radiation counter detects the gamma rays given off by the absorbed I¹³¹. The amount of absorption is known to be related to the physiological activity of the thyroid gland

One can even make stable nuclei unstable. To make an otherwise stable nucleus radioactive, scientists bombard the nucleus with very energetic "bullets." Various elementary particles, especially neutrons, protons, and alpha particles (also known as helium nuclei), have been used as such bullets.

When a nucleus is unstable and also has too much energy, it may break apart into various nuclear fragments through a process called *fission*. It is now possible to control fission very accurately in devices known as NUCLEAR REACTORS.

A less controlled form of fission carried on outside reactors may release immense quantities of heat and other forms of energy almost immediately. This is referred to as a *nuclear explosion*. It may be used as a destructive force in war or for peaceful purposes requiring great amounts of energy.

### ISOTOPES

Somewhat as children assemble pieces of a model kit into various combinations, so do scientists combine protons and neutrons into a great variety of nuclei. Atoms of many elements can be bombarded with neutrons or other particles and converted into other isotopes of the same element or sometimes into different elements. In many cases the new product is radioactive; that is, it is unstable so that it decomposes into some other isotope or element, liberating a particle or form of energy in the process.

Many radioactive isotopes are useful because of the properties of the RADIATION that they emit. Scientists have manufactured several new elements by putting together new combinations of protons, neutrons, and electrons, forming different and more complex combinations than had been known to exist in nature. Of these, PLUTONIUM is one of the better-known synthetic elements, as it is useful in the production of nuclear power. It can be used instead of uranium-235, which occurs in nature.

Certain long-lived radioisotopes are found occurring naturally. They *emit particles at a rate peculiar to each isotope.* Man cannot change this rate or the emanations. Such materials are said to be *naturally radioactive.* Thus there are two types of radioactive materials: *natural* and *man-made*. But

A glandular secretion from frogs, called *bufagin*, is used in treating heart disease. The action of the drug is studied by using radioactive bufagin which is obtained as shown below

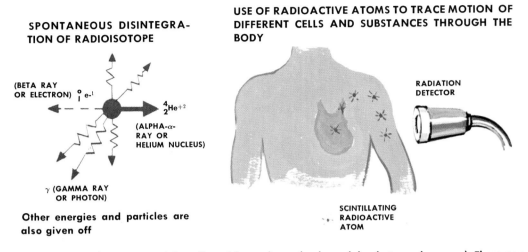

SPONTANEOUS DISINTEGRATION OF RADIOISOTOPE

(BETA RAY OR ELECTRON) $^{0}_{1}e^{-1}$

$^{4}_{2}He^{+2}$

(ALPHA-α-RAY OR HELIUM NUCLEUS)

γ (GAMMA RAY OR PHOTON)

Other energies and particles are also given off

USE OF RADIOACTIVE ATOMS TO TRACE MOTION OF DIFFERENT CELLS AND SUBSTANCES THROUGH THE BODY

RADIATION DETECTOR

SCINTILLATING RADIOACTIVE ATOM

Radioactive atoms disintegrate, giving off particles and rays (such as alpha, beta, and gamma). These particles and rays, invisible to man, are detected by Geiger-Müller counters, even when in very small amounts. Radioactive atoms can mix with regular atoms and circulate through the body. Radiation detectors, moving over the body surface, can trace paths of radioactive atoms. This gives us important medical information.

since radioactive materials found in nature are limited in both amount and type of radioactivity, man-made radioactive materials have become much more important and useful than the natural sort. Radioactive isotopes of nearly all elements are being produced, and new and important uses for these are developing.

Various fragments produced when nuclei break apart include alpha particles, beta particles, protons, neutrons, and gamma rays. When a heavy nucleus, such as one of radium or uranium, decays, one of the fragments is identical to the nucleus of a helium atom. That is, HELIUM is a product of the decay of RADIUM and of uranium. Helium nuclei produced by this process are called *alpha particles.* In other cases, electrons are given off by nuclei as they decompose. These electrons are known as *beta particles.* Discovery of these processes has helped man learn about the structure of atoms and about the nature of the individual particles that make up atoms. Much has been learned, also, about forms of energy such as gamma rays, which have no mass at all.

Radiation is energy moving from one place to another. There are different forms of radiation, of which gamma rays are one. Gamma rays are *electromagnetic rays* like X rays, except in their origin. X rays are produced by electrons outside atomic nuclei. Gamma rays may come from inside or outside. Neutrons, protons, electrons, and

alpha particles, when ejected at very high velocities from nuclei, are also considered as radiation. They have properties of both matter and energy, as they have mass in addition to the energy, which is due to their motion.

USES OF NUCLEAR ENERGY

Nuclear energy is best known as a source of heat for generating electricity or as the ultimate explosive for military battle. There are many other uses for nuclear energy, however, that are not only less well known, but also less controversial. For example, the energy released during the natural decay of many radioactive isotopes (radioisotopes) is being used as a miniature beacon in science and medicine. Because the HALF-LIFE (the rate at which half of any quantity of a radioisotope decays) is constant and because the way the isotope decays is constant, researchers can direct sensitive monitors to look for the specific radiation emitted as an isotope decays. In practice, a nonradioactive substance is "tagged" with a small amount of a radioisotope. The radioisotope will travel with the substance to which it has been tagged. By watching for the tag's radiation, one can essentially watch where the original substance has gone and in what quantities.

Doctors sometimes tag drugs administered to animals and human patients. Then with radiation detectors, physicians monitor where the drug travels through the body, how quickly it travels, whether it accumulates in one place more than another, and whether or not it completely exits the body. Similarly, in the movement of petroleum through long pipelines from the oil-producing areas to refineries, shipments can be identified within the pipe by detecting the radioisotope tags injected at the start.

Over the years, one particular radioisotope has been extremely useful in helping determine the age of wood from ancient times. Cosmic rays, which are nuclear particles coming to the earth from outer space, interact with the upper layers of the atmosphere to form a radioisotope of carbon, known as *carbon-14*. It is formed in definite amounts and through natural processes reaches the soil and becomes part of growing plants at a known rate. The rate of decay of this particular radioisotope is such that after even thousands of years some of it remains in wood or similar plant tissues. By measuring the radioactivity of a sample of wood and comparing it with a piece of wood that was quite recently growing, an estimate of its age can be made.

A newer method of measuring even older items employs detecting atoms of radioactive potassium-40. It decays with a half-life of one billion years to stable argon-40. Potassium-40 is found along with normal potassium in the human body and in most common rocks, especially granite. Its decay rate is so extremely slow that scientists have been able to place the date of manlike fossils back to 1,800,000 years ago using this method.

Radiation kills cells that are growing or dividing rapidly. This fact is being used successfully to destroy tumors and CANCER cells inside the body with relatively little danger to other normal cells. Radioisotopes may be used for this purpose, or a beam of particles from an ACCELERATOR may be directed at the tissue that is to be destroyed.

Radiation doses too small to kill may induce genetic changes that can be used for the betterment of mankind. When living cells are subjected to nonlethal doses of radiation, the genes of the cell, which are important in transmitting characteristic properties of the cell to its descendants, may be changed. The new daughter cells may have new characteristics unlike those of the parent. These are known as *mutations*. In controlled experiments, scientists have been able to encourage inherited changes in plants and animals through radiation treatment. For example, during several generations of irradiating some plants and insects, it was possible to stimulate mutations and to select and reproduce those changes that were desirable. A rust-resistant strain of oats was developed in one and one-half years through radiation-induced mutation; had usual plant-breeding methods been used, it might have required 10 years to find a similar rust-resistant strain.

The same cobalt-60 gamma-radiation source used to kill cancer cells in human patients also shows great promise as a food preservative and pest killer. Food irradiation involves passing gamma rays through foods to sterilize them. The radiation doses delivered to the food—and any bacteria or pests residing on them—would prove lethal. Since the gamma radiation does not make the irradiated food radioactive, nor heat nor change its physical state, the food can be packaged following treatment and stored for years at room temperature without spoilage. Irradiating fresh fruit would also kill any pests, such as the Mediterranean fruit fly, that might otherwise be transmitted as fruit was transported to market.

Finally, neutrons from a reactor can help police detectives in criminal investigations. In one case, a millionaire's "suicide" was ruled a murder when *neutron-activation analysis* proved that the gunshot victim had not fired the revolver found in his hand. Neutron-activation analysis is an extremely sensitive and accurate method of identifying what chemical elements are present in an analyzed sample. To do this, the sample is made radioactive by bombarding it with neutrons. The resulting radioactive sample emits characteristic radiations (such as X rays) that uniquely identify which elements are in the sample and how many atoms of them are present.

When testing persons suspected of firing a gun, investigators swab the back of the hand for traces of gunshot residue. Trace amounts of barium or antimony—common in gunshot residue—can later be matched against levels found on the gun. The absence of such residues on the alleged suicide victim helped police track down the real murderer.                    R.C.S.

SEE ALSO: BOMBS; ELEMENTS; NUCLEAR ENERGY; NUCLEAR PARTICLES; NUCLEAR SCIENCE GLOSSARY; RADIATION, USES OF; RAY, GAMMA

**ACCELERATOR**\*—An electromagnetic device for giving high velocity to elementary particles. Special types include betatrons, bevatrons, cyclotrons, synchrotrons, and Van de Graaff generators.

**ALPHA PARTICLE (RAY)**\*—A positively charged particle given off by some radioactive elements. It is the nucleus of a helium atom and made of two neutrons and two protons.

**ATOM**\*—The material particle or unit of a given chemical element having protons (+) and neutrons in a compact nucleus with electrons (—) moving about the nucleus. The unit, as a whole, is electrically neutral. Atoms cannot be split by chemical changes.

**ATOMIC MASS UNIT (amu)**—One twelfth of the mass of an atom of carbon-12 isotope unit for atomic mass.

**ATOMIC NUMBER**—The number of protons in a nucleus unique for each of the 105 chemical elements.

**BETA PARTICLE (RAY)**\*—An electron ejected from an unstable nucleus; electrons are (—), their antiparticles—positrons—are (+).

**CATHODE RAYS**—A stream of electrons from the negative electrode of a gas or a radio or TV tube.

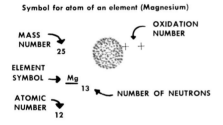

Symbol for atom of an element (Magnesium)

MASS NUMBER 25

OXIDATION NUMBER

ELEMENT SYMBOL → Mg

ATOMIC NUMBER 12

13 ← NUMBER OF NEUTRONS

**CHAIN REACTION**—A self-sustaining reaction such as when neutrons are released by fission at a rate causing more fission.

**COSMIC RAYS**—High-energy particles and radiation from outer space; most are high-speed protons.

**CRITICAL MASS**—The amount of nuclear fuel necessary to initiate a nuclear chain reaction.

**CURIE**—A basic unit of radioactivity named for Marie Curie. It equals 37 billion disintegrations per second, which is roughly the activity associated with one gram of radium. It is also the mass of any material having 1 Curie of activity.

**DECAY**—The disintegrations that occur as one radioactive (unstable) element stabilizes into others by shedding particles and energy.

**DEUTERIUM**—An isotope of hydrogen, symbol $^2_1$H.

**ELECTROMAGNETIC RADIATION**—Radiation with zero rest mass that travels through empty space and, in some forms, through matter. Depending on its wavelength, this radiation is known as gamma, ultraviolet, or X rays; visible light; or infrared, radio or microwaves.

**ELECTRON**\*—An elementary particle carrying one unit of negative electric charge. In its natural state, it orbits about an atomic nucleus. It has a mass 1/1837 that of a proton.

**ELEMENT**\*—A substance the particles of which cannot be divided by chemical changes; atoms of one element have the same atomic number.

**ENERGY**\*—The capacity to do work.

**FALLOUT**—Airborne particles with radioactive materials, falling to earth after a nuclear explosion.

**FISSION**—The breaking apart of a heavy nucleus into two nearly equal parts, accompanied by the release of roughly 200 million electron volts of energy and two or more neutrons.

**FLUX (NEUTRON)**—The intensity of neutron radiation, expressed as the number hitting a unit area of target per second.

**FUEL (NUCLEAR)**—A material that will fission, releasing energy in a nuclear reactor.

**GAMMA RAYS**\*—The highest energy (shortest wavelength) electromagnetic radiation. They are similar to—often indistinguishable from—X rays and are emitted by the decay of radioactive elements.

**GEIGER-MÜLLER COUNTER**\*—An instrument for detecting and measuring intensity of radiation; it does this indirectly by electronically registering ions formed.

**HALF-LIFE**\*—The time it takes for one half of a given radioactive element to decay. (See DECAY.)

**HOT**—Highly radioactive.

**HYDROGEN BOMB**—A fusion weapon. A fission bomb (atomic bomb) is needed to set it off. Its size can be unlimited.

**INTENSITY**—Concentration of ENERGY hitting a surface of unit area in unit time.

**IONIZING RADIATION**—*Elementary particles* that knock electrons from or give electrons to atoms, leaving them charged positively or negatively. A charged atom is called an *ion*.

**IRRADIATE**—To expose to radiation.

**MANHATTAN PROJECT**—A top-secret War Department program during World War II to develop nuclear-fission (atomic) bombs under General Leslie Groves. In 1947 it was taken over by the U.S. Atomic Energy Commission.

**MASS ENERGY EQUATION**—Einstein's equation, $E=mc^2$, states that the moving *mass* times the

\*Special articles of this title appear in this Encyclopedia.

velocity of *light* squared equals the *energy* equivalent of this mass. It holds that energy and mass can be interchangeable. It is the basic equation for changes in nuclear energy, developed as the Special Theory of *Relativity* by *Einstein* in 1905.

MUON—*Elementary particle*; class, *lepton*; mass 207 electron masses; also called mu meson.

NEUTRINO—An *elementary particle*; no mass or electric charge; has spin and energy; can pass through the earth.

NEUTRON—An uncharged elementary particle with a mass roughly equal to a proton's and associated with protons in the nuclei of all atoms heavier than hydrogen. Neutrons are not ejected by radioactive decay but are ejected from nuclei in some nuclear reactions, such as fission.

NUCLEAR REACTION—Changes in atomic nuclei by *radioactive decay*, *fission*, or *fusion*.

NUCLEONS—Parts of nuclei; either protons or neutrons.

PAIR PRODUCTION—The transformation of energy to mass (an electron and a positron), which occurs when a gamma ray (with energy greater than 1.02 million electron volts) passes through the intense electric field outside an atomic nucleus. It is the opposite of pair annihilation. In pair annihilation, electrons and positrons unite to form gamma rays.

PARTICLE, ELEMENTARY—The building blocks of chemical elements and the universe; includes electrons, neutrons, photons, protons, and more than 100 more.

PERSONNEL MONITORING—Safety procedures to measure the amount of nuclear radiation. Persons can carry film badges, dosimeters, or pass through detecting stations.

PLASMA (ionic)—A nearly neutral, ionized gas, as in a neon light and the solar corona.

POSITRON—An elementary particle with (+) electric charge and with the same mass as one electron, its antiparticle.

QUANTUM THEORY—One important basis for modern physics and chemistry. It states that radiation energy is emitted by oscillating sources in natural bundles of energy (quanta).

QUARK—Any of the elementary subparticles out of which all elementary particles are believed to have been built. They come in sets of three: two will have electric charges of -1/3; the other has a +2/3 charge.

RAD (Radiation Absorbed Dose)—Basic unit of absorbed dose of ionizing radiation, 100 ERGS of radiation ENERGY per gram of absorbing material.

RADIATION WARNING SYMBOL—Official symbol is a magenta trefoil on yellow; it is posted near dangerous radiation.

**RADIATION WARNING SYMBOL**

RADIATION AREA

RADIATION PROTECTION GUIDE—Official allowable radiation doses to avoid unsafe exposure, set by Federal Radiation Council (formerly "maximum permissible dose," MPD).

RADIOISOTOPE·—Isotopes that emit radiation.

REM—(Roentgen Equivalent Man) The absorbed dose of any ionizing radiation producing the same effect (on life) as one rad of absorbed therapeutic X rays.

ROENTGEN—A unit of exposure to ionizing radiation; the amount of gamma or X rays to produce ions having one unit electric charge per cubic centimeter of dry air.

SHIELDING—Material used to reduce or stop dangerous radiation.

SHOCK WAVE—A forceful gust of air, or pulse of earth or water, from a nuclear explosion.

SPARK CHAMBER·—An instrument for detecting and measuring the paths, masses, etc., of elementary particles; related to cloud and bubble chambers.

THERMONUCLEAR REACTION—A fusion reaction; it uses high temperatures to combine two light nuclei to form an atom with a heavier nucleus; it gives out great energy.

TRACER (ISOTOPIC)—A radioactive element put into living, chemical, or physical subjects and then viewed by radiation detectors.

TRANSMUTATION—The changing of one element into another through a nuclear reaction.

TRITIUM—An isotope of hydrogen; symbol $^3_1H$; a useful tracer.

VAN DE GRAAFF GENERATOR—An electrostatic machine that can be used as a particle accelerator. Often it speeds particles for larger accelerators.

X RAY—Electromagnetic waves emitted when high-energy electrons bombard matter.

D.A.B./M.S.P.

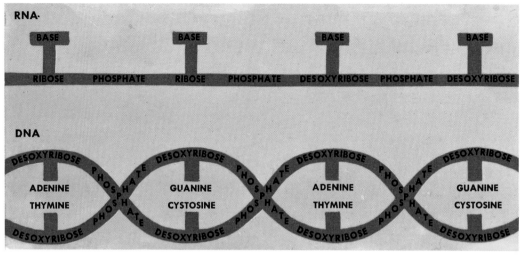

Diagrammatic structures of ribonucleic acid and desoxyribonucleic acid molecules

**Nucleic acid** (nyoo-KLEE-ick) Nucleic acids are chemical compounds found in all plant and animal cells, as well as in bacteria and viruses. There are two types of nucleic acid. DNA (*desoxyribonucleic acid*) is found in the nuclei of cells. RNA (*ribonucleic acid*) is found in the cytoplasm of cells. DNA is believed to be the hereditary material that passes the characteristics of living structures from one generation to the next.

Nucleic acids are normally combined with PROTEINS in the cell to form NUCLEOPROTEINS. The nucleic acid molecule is a combination of various *purine* and *pyrimidine* bases (cytosine, uracil, thymine, adenine, and guanine); a sugar (either desoxyribose or ribose); and phosphoric acid. Two main types are formed.      J. C. K.
SEE ALSO: CELL, CHROMOSOME, GENE, HEREDITY, PURINE, PYRIMIDINE

**Nucleolus** see Cell, Histology

**Nucleon** see Nuclear particles, Nuclear science

**Nucleoprotein** Nucleoproteins are chemical substances located in cells. Since all living things, plants and animals, are made up of cells, nucleoproteins play an important part in all the activities of life. While nucleoprotein is made of *nucleic acid* and *protein,* research has shown that it is the nucleic acid that is responsible for the way in which it functions (works) in the living cell.

The basic unit of the nucleic acid part of nucleoprotein is called *nucleotide*. Chains of nucleotides make up nucleic acids. A nucleotide is made of a sugar-phosphate group joined to either a *pyrimidine* or *purine* group. A *pyrimidine* molecule contains four carbon and two nitrogen atoms joined together in a closed ring. A *purine* molecule consists of two rings, each containing carbon and nitrogen atoms. The sugar in the nucleotide is always one of two kinds—either *ribose* or *desoxyribose* sugar. Both sugars are formed by a chain of five carbon atoms, but desoxyribose differs from ribose because it lacks one oxygen atom. In any nucleic acid only one kind of sugar is present in its nucleotides.

Thus there are two kinds of nucleic acids, depending on which kind of sugar is present. If ribose sugar is present, the nucleic acid is called *ribonucleic acid,* or *RNA* for short. When desoxyribose sugar is present, the nucleic acid is called *desoxyribonucleic acid,* or *DNA,* or *deoxyribonucleic acid.*

A DNA nucleotide may combine with one of two kinds of pyrimidines or with one of two kinds of purines. Therefore there are four possible kinds of nucleotides. Very many of each of these four kinds are united together in different arrangements in order to form a DNA spiral ladder-like molecule.

To summarize:

A.
$$\left.\begin{array}{c} \text{One of two pyrimidines} \\ \text{or} \\ \text{One of two purines} \end{array}\right\} \begin{array}{l} + \text{Ribose sugar} \\ + \text{phosphoric acid} \\ = \text{four kinds of nucleotides} \end{array}$$

B.
$$\left.\begin{array}{c} \text{One of two pyrimidines} \\ \text{or} \\ \text{One of two purines} \end{array}\right\} \begin{array}{l} + \text{Desoxyribose sugar} \\ + \text{phosphoric acid} \\ = \text{four kinds of nucleotides} \end{array}$$

The A nucleotides form ribonucleic acid, or RNA. The B nucleotides form desoxyribonuclei acid, or DNA. DNA or RNA, when added to protein, form nucleoproteins.

### NUCLEOPROTEINS AND HEREDITY

RNA nucleoproteins are found in several places in a cell, but the DNA type is found only in nucleoproteins of chromosomes. GENES are located on chromosomes and may be defined as centers of biochemical action controlling development of inherited traits within an individual. A gene may correspond to a certain segment of chromosomal nucleiprotein. Research has shown that the nucleic acid part of a nucleoprotein is responsible for the development of genetic traits, and it is always composed of DNA. According to present-day theory, the DNA molecules act as a blueprint giving the cells two kinds of information. First, it gives the cell a pattern or template so that the cell can make a new DNA molecule exactly like the original ones. Second, it tells the cell which *amino acids* to join together to make specific proteins. Genetic traits such as blue eyes depend on the presence of specific proteins.

However, it is known that centers for specific protein formation (synthesis) are not in the cell nucleus but in small granules (*ribosomes*) in the cytoplasm of the cell. RNA, the second kind of nucleic acid found in cells, has been shown to be the link between the DNA molecules with their master patterns and the ribosomes, or protein manufacturing centers, in the cytoplasm. RNA is made in the chromosomes and released from the nucleus to make patterns for the proteins formed in the ribosomes.     J. C. K.
SEE ALSO: HEREDITY

**Nucleus** see Atom, Cell, Nuclear particles, Nuclear science

As civilizations became more complicated they developed organized numeral systems.

**Numeral systems** As the quantitative needs of primitive man increased, he found himself faced with questions such as "How many?", "How big?", "How much?". It became necessary for man's early ancestors to devise some kind of a system that they could use to record and to communicate ideas of number and number relationships. An organized system of number names (*numeration*) and number symbols (*notation*) is called a *numeral system*.

A symbol contains no meaning within itself. It gets meaning by common agreement. Which of the following is the number "three"?

▽ ▽ ▽, III, ///, 3, 11₂, Γ, · · ·

It will be shown that all of these are different ways to represent the number "three." For this reason, symbols, like 1, 2, 3, and so on, are called *numerals*. These are the number names that a *numeral* system must start with.

The systems of notation are of two chief types: *non-positional* systems and *positional* systems.

### NON-POSITIONAL:
### SIMPLE GROUPING SYSTEMS

One of the simplest systems devised by man is the simple grouping system. To represent a given number, symbols are repeated and their values added. (Some writers refer to such a system as an "additive" one.) The early Egyptian system is a good example of a simple grouping system.

VALUE  SYMBOL

| VALUE | SYMBOL | |
|---|---|---|
| 1 | I | stroke |
| 10 | ∩ | arch |
| 100 | ୧ | coiled rope |
| 1,000 | ⚘ | lotus flower |
| 10,000 | ⟨ | pointed finger |
| 100,000 | ⌒ | tadpole |
| 1,000,000 | 𓀠 | astonished man |

The seven symbols used in the early Egyptian system and the numerical values of each in the Hindu-Arabic system are shown above. The Egyptians represented 1,246 and 32,488 as:

1,246          32,488

Sometimes the Egyptians wrote their numerals from left to right—the largest to the left, the smallest to the right. Often they reversed this and had the smallest unit at the left. Notice how 257 might appear in both cases:

The way fractions were treated made this system exceedingly awkward to use. Every fraction numeral (with the exception of ⅔) had to be expressed with a numerator of 1—all unit fractions. The symbol ○ stood for a numerator of 1. Here are some of the commonly used fractions in this system of notation:

1/8          1/3          1/10          1/12

$\dfrac{7}{12}$ was expressed as (symbols) because

$$\frac{7}{12} = \frac{1}{3} + \frac{1}{4}$$

As difficult as the Egyptian system was to use, it served its purpose. The early Egyptians were very practical people. Their chief need for a system of numeration was to measure their fields, divide their crops, pay their taxes, build their temples, pyramids, and tombs. It had shortcomings—difficult notation, awkwardness of computation, treatment of fractions—but served its *purpose*.

The Roman numeral system was also a simple grouping system. The seven symbols used in writing Roman numerals and the numerical value of each in the Hindu-Arabic system are shown below:

| Symbol | I | V | X | L | C | D | M |
|---|---|---|---|---|---|---|---|
| Value | 1 | 5 | 10 | 50 | 100 | 500 | 1,000 |

When a symbol was repeated, its value was added.

III = 3; XXX = 30; CCC = 300;
MMM = 3,000

When a symbol was written to the left of a symbol of greater value, its value was subtracted from the larger symbol.

IV = 4     XL = 40     CD = 400

When a symbol was written to the right of a symbol of equal or greater value, its value was added to the value of the equal or greater value.

LIX = 59  DXXX = 530  MCM = 1900

A horizontal bar over a symbol multiplied the value of the symbol by 1,000.

$\overline{XV} = 10,005$     $\overline{M} = 1,000,000$
$\overline{X}CLIV = 10,154$

Computation involving such a numeral system was most confusing and tedious. To further complicate the system, to express fractions a base 12 system was used.

The Roman numeral system along with computation on the Roman abacus was so strongly entrenched that people were reluctant to accept the Hindu-Arabic system when it was first introduced in Europe, around 1200. It took about 400 years before it was widely accepted.

## NON-POSITIONAL:
### MULTIPLICATIVE GROUPING SYSTEMS

A multiplicative grouping system uses two sets of symbols: one set for $1, 2, 3, \cdots, (n-1)$, and the other for $n, n^2, n^3, \cdots$. For example, in a decimal multiplicative grouping system, the first set could be $1, 2, 3, \cdots, 7, 8, 9$ and the other set could be A for 10, B for $10^2$, C for $10^3$, D for $10^4$, etc. Then 4,857 would be expressed as 4C 8B 5A 7; 15,206 would be expressed as 1D 5C 2B 6.

The Chinese-Japanese numeration system is a multiplicative grouping system. The two sets of symbols are:

一 二 三 四 五 六 七 八 九
1　2　3　4　5　6　7　8　9　and
十　　百　　千
10　　$10^2$　　$10^3$

Observe how 4,921 would be written in this system and the vertical arrangement of the numerals.

四千九百二十一
$4 \times 1000$
$9 \times 100$
$2 \times 10$
$1 \times 1$

## NON-POSITIONAL
### CIPHERED NUMERAL SYSTEMS

In a ciphered numeral system of notation, several sets of symbols are necessary.

first set:  $1, \quad 2, \quad 3, \cdots, (n-1)$
second set:  $n, 2n, 3n, \cdots, (n-1)n$
third set:  $n^2, 2n^2, 3n^2, \cdots, (n-1)n^2$
fourth set:  $n^3, 2n^3, 3n^3, \cdots, (n-1)n^3$

A Greek numeral system, known as the Ionic, which flourished around 450 B.C., was an example of a ciphered numeral system.

| | | | | | | | | | |
|---|---|---|---|---|---|---|---|---|---|
| first set | A | B | Γ | Δ | E | F | Z | H | θ |
| | 1 | 2 | 3 | 4 | 5 | 6 | 7 | 8 | 9 |
| second set | I | K | Λ | M | N | Ξ | O | Π | ¶ |
| | 10 | 20 | 30 | 40 | 50 | 60 | 70 | 80 | 90 |
| third set | P | Σ | T | γ | Φ | X | Ψ | Ω | ⅄ |
| | 100 | 200 | 300 | 400 | 500 | 600 | 700 | 800 | 900 |

Other examples of ciphered numeral systems were those used by the Hebrews, the Syrians, and the early Hindus.

## POSITIONAL SYSTEMS

A positional system employs one set of symbols. Each symbol stands for a cardinal number on its own. To express numbers which are larger than the base employed, two or more of these basic symbols (not necessarily distinct) are needed. For a positional system, base $= n$

Symbols: $0, 1, 2, 3, \cdots, (n-1), n$
Base Values
$\cdots \mid n^4 \mid n^3 \mid n^2 \mid n \mid$

The Mayan system of notation is a fine example of a positional system.

| Symbols | 1 | 2 | 3 | 4 | 5 | 6 | 7 | 8 |
|---|---|---|---|---|---|---|---|---|
| | 9 | 10 | 11 | 12 | 13 | 14 | 15 | 16 | 17 | 18 | 19 |

This system was used by the Mayan Indians of Yucatan. With dots and strokes they could represent any number from one to nineteen. With the symbol ⬭ which they wrote immediately below any one of their basic symbols, they made the symbol twenty times larger $180 =$ ⬭

They wrote their numerals vertically with the smallest size units at the bottom. Note how they expressed 345 and 166.

$17 \times 20$
$5 \times 1$

$8 \times 20$
$6 \times 1$

The Babylonians like the Egyptians employed symbols for one and ten. Y stood for one, and ◁ stood for ten. The system was a base 60 system, so each base position represented an integral power of 60. For numbers smaller than 60 they used an additive principle.

34 was expressed as ◁◁◁ YY YY

51 was expressed as ◁◁◁◁◁ Y

For numbers greater than 60 they employed positional notation.

77 was represented as Y ◁ YYY YYYY
because $77 = 1 \times 60 + 17$

1,355 was shown as ◁◁ YY ◁◁◁ YY YYY
because $1,355 = 22 \times 60 + 35$

Unfortunately the same set of symbols could also represent 81,300, or $\frac{2122}{3600}$, or many others. This was the result of difficulty in determining the base position in which a cluster of symbols appeared. Also in the absence of a symbol for zero, a gap in between symbols stood for a zero. But it was difficult to tell if a gap were intended or merely a separation of base positions.

$$\triangledown \quad \triangledown \text{ could stand for}$$
$$1 \times 60^2 + 0 \times 60 + 1 = 3601$$

or for

$$1 + \frac{0}{60} + \frac{1}{3600} = 1 \frac{1}{3600}.$$

The system in universal use today is called the *Hindu-Arabic numeral system*. In its present form it has been used less than 500 years. All numerals are formed by using one or more of the ten symbols, 1,2,3,4,5,6, 7,8,9,0 called digits.

The chart below shows the place values for the decimal units from ones to hundred thousands. Note that each decimal unit is ten times larger as one moves from right to left, and one-tenth as large as one goes from left to right.

Hundred thousands . . . . . . . . . . . . $10^5$
Ten thousands . . . . . . . . . . . . . . . $10^4$
Thousands . . . . . . . . . . . . . . . . . $10^3$
Hundreds . . . . . . . . . . . . . . . . . . $10^2$
Tens . . . . . . . . . . . . . . . . . . . . . $10^1$
Ones . . . . . . . . . . . . . . . . . . . . . $10^0$

The greatest digit one can write in any decimal base position of course is 9 because each ten units is always replaced by one unit 10 times as great. A zero in any base position indicates the absence of any units in that base position.

The numeral 11,111 stands for 1 one, 1 ten, 1 hundred, 1 thousand, and 1 ten-thousand, $5,802 = (5 \times 10^3) + (8 \times 10^2) + (0 \times 10^1) + (2 \times 10^0)$.

Any numeral N may be expressed in polynominal form as

$$N = a_0 10^n + a_1 10^{n-1} + \cdots + a_{n-1} 10^1 + a_n 10^0 + \cdots$$

where the coefficients $a_0, a_1, a_2, \ldots, a_{n-1}, a_n,$ $\cdots$ are taken from the set $0,1,2,\cdots, 8,9$ and the exponent n is an integer. If the exponents are all positive integers or zero, then N is an integer. If some or all of the exponents are negative integers, then a mixed number or decimal fraction results.

$$2.783 = 2 \times 10^0 + 7 \times 10^{-1} + 8 \times 10^{-2} + 3 \times 10^{-3}$$

The Hindu-Arabic system is a decimal system, base 10, most likely because man has 10 fingers. But any natural number (other than 1) could serve as a base. Because of the application of binary numbers (base 2)

to high speed computers and other problems, binary numbers will be discussed briefly.

The "digits" in a base 2 system can only be 1 and 0. If one counts in base 2, symbols for numbers will look like this: 1, 10, 11, 100, 101, 110, 111, 1000, etc. An analysis of the place value chart below is helpful in understanding it.

Sixty-fours . . . . . . . . . . . . . . . . . $2^6$
Thirty-twos . . . . . . . . . . . . . . . . . $2^5$
Sixteens . . . . . . . . . . . . . . . . . . . $2^4$
Eights . . . . . . . . . . . . . . . . . . . . $2^3$
Fours . . . . . . . . . . . . . . . . . . . . . $2^2$
Twos . . . . . . . . . . . . . . . . . . . . . $2^1$
Ones . . . . . . . . . . . . . . . . . . . . . $2^0$

The smallest units of quantity are $2^0$ or ones; then $2^1$ or twos; followed by $2^2$ or fours; $2^3$ or eights; $2^4$ or sixteens; $2^5$ or thirty-twos, etc. 27 base 10—written $27_{10}$—when expressed in base 2 is 11011 (1 sixteen, 1 eight, no fours, 1 two and 1 one). $27_{10} = 11011_2$. $301_{10} = ?_2$. One can divide 301 successively by 2, paying particular attention to the remainders.

```
2 ⌐ 301
  2 ⌐ 150    R    1    ↑
    2 ⌐ 75   R    0
      2 ⌐ 37   R    1
        2 ⌐ 18   R    1
          2 ⌐ 9   R    0
            2 ⌐ 4   R    1
              2 ⌐ 2   R    0
                2 ⌐ 1   R    0
                    0   R    1
```

The remainders are read upward and one concludes that $301_{10} = 100101101_2$. The accuracy can be checked:

$$
\begin{array}{rcl}
1 \times 256 &=& 256 \\
0 \times 128 &=& \\
0 \times 64 &=& \\
1 \times 32 &=& 32 \\
0 \times 16 &=& \\
1 \times 8 &=& 8 \\
1 \times 4 &=& 4 \\
0 \times 2 &=& \\
1 \times 1 &=& 1 \\
\hline
 & & 301
\end{array}
$$

For addition only one "fact" is needed: $1 + 1 = 10$. Similarly, for multiplication $1 \times 1 = 1$. Of course, the zero properties for addition and multiplication hold as with base $_{10}$.

**Nuthatch**

Add $1110_2$ and $111_2$

$$
\begin{array}{ll}
1110 & 0+1=1 \\
\underline{\phantom{1}111} & 1+1=10;\ \text{write 0, remember 1} \\
10101 & 1+1+1=11;\ \text{write 1,} \\
& \quad \text{remember 1}
\end{array}
$$

$1+1=10$

Multiply $1101_2$ by $101_2$:

$$
\begin{array}{r}
1101 \\
\underline{101} \\
1101 \\
1101\phantom{0} \\
\hline
1000001
\end{array}
$$

Now, let us return to the number "three."

▽ ▽▽ , III, ///, 3, 11₂, Γ, · · ·

represent "three" in Mayan, Roman, Egyptian, Hindu-Arabic, base 2, and Greek systems, respectively.       I.K.F./M.M.L.
SEE ALSO: ALGEBRA, ARITHMETIC, MATHEMATICS, STATISTICS

**Nursery** see Horticulture

**Nutcracker** Nutcrackers are crow-like birds. They are often called *Clark crows*. They collect nuts, almonds, pine cones, and other hard fruits, and store them for future use. They use their strong beaks to crack the nuts before they eat the seeds. Nutcrackers have heavy, curved and sharply-pointed claws that are useful in clinging to branches.

The European nutcracker lives in central Europe. It is found in the mountains near the timber line. It is brown and has white spots. It prefers the cones of the pine trees for food.

The nutcracker of western North America is a pale gray with black and white wings and a white throat.       M. R. L.
SEE ALSO: BIRD NESTS

Nutcracker

**Nuthatch** The nuthatch is a small bird. It has a long, straight bill, a short, square tail and large feet and claws. It hunts its food—insects, insect eggs or seeds—among cracks in tree bark and can walk sideways or up and down on a tree trunk or branch. Nuthatches build twig and grass nests in holes in trees.

The *red-breasted nuthatch* is a small bird about 4½ inches (11.4 centimeters) long. It lives in pine forests and eats pine seeds. It has a black cap and reddish-brown underparts. Its call is short and nasal.

The *white-breasted nuthatch* is one of the most abundant winter residents in eastern America. It has a blue-gray back and white breast. It prefers open woods to forests.

The *pygmy nuthatch,* a gray bird, is a western bird, and the *brown-headed nuthatch* lives in southern pine woods.       E. R. B.

**Nutmeg** Nutmeg is the dried seed or nut found inside the kernel of the fruit of the tropical evergreen nutmeg tree. The tree is native to the Spice Islands.

The grayish-brown nutmegs, round or oval, have a pleasantly pungent aroma. Ground nutmeg adds a warm, bitter, yet delicious flavor to foods and beverages.

The groves of tall nutmeg trees look much like orange groves with their many blossoms and small, round, green fruits which turn golden yellow when ripe.

When the fruit opens, there is a bright red membrane covering part of the nut. *Mace,* another spice, comes from this membrane. Both the seed and covering give an oil used in medicine and cosmetics.       J. K. K.
SEE ALSO: MACE

**Nutmeg**

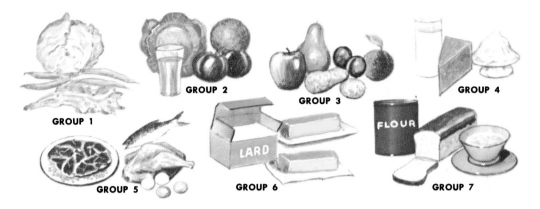

GROUP 1

GROUP 2

GROUP 3

GROUP 4

GROUP 5

GROUP 6

GROUP 7

**Nutrition** (new-TRIH-shun) Nutrition includes all the processes by which a plant or animal obtains food and uses it. All substances which an organism can use to build protoplasm and produce energy are foods. Plants produce their own food from CARBON DIOXIDE, WATER, and minerals through PHOTOSYNTHESIS. The foods of animals include organic materials made by plants or other animals, and water and minerals. Organic foods are of four types: CARBOHYDRATES, which include sugar and starches; PROTEINS; FATS; and VITAMINS. All animals, except a few parasites, must capture their food. There are seven basic types of food needed for health.

Once an animal catches its food, it is digested or broken down into substances which are then distributed to the body cells. In man, water, water-soluble vitamins, and minerals need no digestion. Fat-soluble vitamins and digested fats are absorbed into lymph vessels in the small intestine. These vessels eventually join the CIRCULATORY SYSTEM. Digested carbohydrates and proteins enter the capillaries in the small intestine.

Good nutrition depends upon getting adequate, but not excessive, amounts of every type of food. Among the necessary minerals are CALCIUM and PHOSPHORUS needed for tooth and bone growth, IRON needed for red blood cells, SODIUM and POTASSIUM needed for proper heartbeat, and IODINE for thyroxin, a metabolic hormone. Traces of other minerals such as copper are also needed.

Water makes up about seventy per cent of the tissues of the body. It is constantly lost from the body and must be replaced.

Vitamins also play an important part in body functions. A certain amount of each of the kinds of vitamins seems to be important in maintaining the health of certain parts of the body or functions. Vitamins, minerals, and water are needed in smaller amounts than the other foods.

The human body must have proteins in order to grow, repair tissues, produce hormones and disease-fighting antibodies. All organic foods can supply energy to the body. The most readily usable form of energy is provided by carbohydrate foods. However, one tablespoon of fat provides two and one-quarter times as much energy as a tablespoon of carbohydrates. Carbohydrates are the only food which can be almost totally eliminated from the diet.     J. K. L.

SEE ALSO: DIGESTIVE SYSTEM, MALNUTRITION, METABOLISM, ORGANIC COMPOUNDS, VITAMIN, VITAMIN DEFICIENCIES

**Nuts** In the true classification of fruits, a nut is dry, has a single seed and a hard shell, and does not open when it is ripe. Acorn, hazelnut, and hickory are true nuts. Almond, cashew, and peanut are not. Any hard-shelled FRUIT that can be dried and stored for a long period of time is commonly called a nut.

Tall, deciduous, and sometimes evergreen oak trees produce acorn fruit. The nut is in a cup-shaped involucre. Acorns are high in carbohydrate. Beechnut trees, 100 feet (30.5 meters) tall, produce several three-sided, small nuts in a spiny-

SEED COAT

MEAT

PERICARP

PECAN

BRAZIL NUT

ENGLISH
WALNUT

ALMOND
(NOT A TRUE NUT)
PRICKLY HUSK

CHESTNUT          SEED COAT

coated fruit. Hazelnut shrubs or trees range in size from 10 to 100 feet (3 to 30.5 meters) high. One species in this group is the filbert. It has round or long brown nuts.

Brazil nuts grow in the Amazon forests. This 150-foot (45.7-meter) tree develops 6 inch (15.25 centimeters) round fruit with a thick woody wall. Each fruit may contain 18 to 24 triangular "nuts." Fleshy seeds inside the nuts contain 70 percent fat.

Nuts of tall shagbark hickory trees are over an inch (2.5 centimeters) long. Bitternut and pignut are kinds of hickories, but their fruit is not edible. Hawaii grows thousands of macadamia trees. Their nuts are rich in oil. The water chestnut is an aquatic herb with a four angled, nutlike fruit. Pistachio, or green almond, is a small tree. Its fruit is a drupe; the nuts are seeds.

The 100-foot (30.5-meter) pecan tree is grown in southern states, for it is not too hardy. Its nuts contain over 70 percent oil. There are three main kinds of deciduous walnut trees—the black, white, and English species. The hull of the black walnut leaves a permanent brown stain. English walnuts are very thin-shelled.

Almond trees are about 12 feet (3.7 meters) tall. They produce a small, peachlike fruit. The nut, inside the drupe, is very high in protein. Cashew nuts come from a 40-foot (12.2-meter) evergreen tree. A curved nut or seed the size of a kidney bean is fastened at the end of a red or yellow fleshy fruit. The peanut, also called goober, is a 1- to 2-foot (.3- to .6-meter) annual herb.

Nuts are considered almost a well-balanced diet. They are high in protein and fat and have some sugar, starch, and minerals. Man is finding an increasing number of uses for nuts. This factor, plus the readiness with which nut trees can be planted in areas not suited for other types of agriculture, has brought about an increased interest in their production. Experimenters are selecting and hybridizing many new varieties.     H.J.C.

SEE ALSO: ECONOMIC BOTANY, FRUIT

**Nylon** Nylon is an artificial material made from air, coal, water, and petroleum and plant chemicals. Unlike cotton which grows on a plant, nylon is made in a laboratory or factory.

Because nylon is strong, it is used for rugs, tubing, fishing lines and PARACHUTES. Broad fibers of nylon make long-wearing brush bristles. It stretches well and thus makes stockings that fit readily.

Nylon was developed in 1938 by a chemist, Dr. Wallace H. Carothers at Du Pont Company. He combined two organic chemicals—*hexamethylene-diamine* and *adipic acid* by forming POLYMERS of them. Du Pont engineers then had to devise ways to produce in quantity these two, formerly rare chemicals. They finally succeeded in making them from common materials (gases of air, etc.).

To carry on the synthesis, the two compounds are heated by steam, then put under pressure. The semi-solid nylon comes out as a flabby sheet that is ice-cooled to harden it. It can next be chopped into bits and stored. Fiber is made from the bits by reheating and thus melting them in an oxidation-preventing atmosphere (as in nitrogen gas). This melted nylon is forced through fine holes to come out as fibers. A twisting and stretching process then lines up the nylon molecules to give a strong final product.     P. G. B.

SEE ALSO: SYNTHETIC FABRICS

**Nymph**  see Metamorphosis

**Oak tree, leaf and acorn**

**A desert oasis**

Buchsbaum

**Oak** The mighty oak is a strong tree. The trunk is large and holds many sturdy branches. The roots go deep into the soil to keep the tree upright. Oaks are very important hardwoods in North America. They give shade, beauty and timber.

Oak leaves are simple, pinnately veined and usually lobed. The small flowers are pollinated by the wind. The fruit (acorn) is classified as a nut. The acorns of the *white oaks* will ripen and germinate in one year. It takes two years for the *black oak* species to accomplish the same process.

The western oaks are not as valuable for lumber as the eastern varieties. The bark is high in tannin, which is extracted for use in treating leather. The eastern oaks include the following kinds. The *red oak* is the largest, growing over 100 feet (30.5 meters). The *scarlet oak* leaves turn bright red in fall. The *live oak* has evergreen leaves. The *bur oak* has large nuts which are eaten by animals. The *blackjack oak* leaves form a triangle. There are about 200 kinds of oak. H.J.C.

**Oarfish** These are deep-sea fish and one species of the ribbonfish. They may be 30 feet (9.1 meters) long. Beginning with a plume-like crest, the dorsal fin runs the entire length of the body.

**Oarfish**

**Oasis** (oh-AY-siss) An oasis is a place in the DESERT where there is water enough for plants and animals and sometimes for a human population. The water comes mainly from springs.

**Oat plant and grain**

**Oat** Oats are a cereal grain planted in the northern states. It may grow wild. The leaves are bluish-green on a stem up to 5 feet (1.5 meters) tall.

Spring oats require wet, cool and even cloudy weather. Winter oats need to be grown in regions where the winters are not severe. They will do well in heavy, even poor, soils as long as they have plenty of water.

Oats contain more protein, fat and minerals than other grains. However, it lacks gluten which is desirable in the flour necessary to make light bread. Man also uses oats as livestock feed, a nurse and hay crop, and straw bedding for livestock quarters.

The flower is an inflorescence with some plants having as many as 60 hanging on upright spikelets. Threshing does not remove all of the pericarp or fruit wall, which limits the quality of flour extracted from the starchy endosperm. The material left is called *groat*. H.J.C.

**Obesity** (oh-BEE-sih-tee) People who weigh over ten to twenty per cent more than they should for their height, age, and body build are obese. Obesity is an imbalance of metabolism (body chemistry). It may be caused by overeating, by malfunction of body glands, or by breakdown of the body tissues.

Obesity injures the body in many ways. The body must keep itself in balance in order to work properly. This balance is called *homeostasis*. When a person is obese, large masses of fat are stored throughout the body. This fat requires extra blood vessels to keep it nourished. The additional blood supply and weight that must be supported increase the amount of work of the heart in pumping blood. When the load becomes too great, heart disease, high blood pressure, and kidney disorders appear.

As the body increases in mass, more energy is needed to keep it alive. However, the balance of storing and burning up food in body cells becomes greatly disturbed. Food is stored as fat instead of being used as a source of energy, and the obese patient may actually suffer from malnutrition and starvation.

The feeling of hunger is controlled by nerve centers in the *hypothalamus,* a part of the brain very close to the PITUITARY gland. The normal function of hunger is to signal a person to take in food when the body senses the absence of food in the stomach. If more food is consistently taken in than is necessary to fulfill the needs of the body, obesity will result.

A reducing plan for an obese person must be entrusted to a physician. If obesity remains untreated, the life span is greatly shortened by breakdown of the organs under so heavy a burden.                     B. B. G.
SEE ALSO: HOMEOSTASIS, NUTRITION

**Observatory** (uhb-ZER-va-toe-re) An observatory is a special type of building where astronomers watch and study the stars, planets, moon, and other heavenly bodies. Observatories are made in such a way that the openings

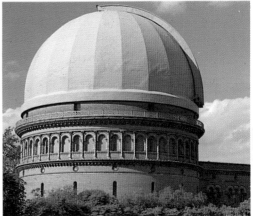

James P. Rowan

**Yerkes Observatory in Williams Bay, Wisconsin has the largest refracting telescope in the world.**

to the sky can be turned so that the TELESCOPES and other instruments can face all points in the sky. Radio observatories have huge saucer-shaped devices which are used to pick up electromagnetic signals from space. The world's largest reflecting telescope, with a segmented mirror 400 inches (1,016 cm) in diameter, is at the Keck Observatory in Hawaii.

There are other types of observatories other than those that are used in the study of heavenly bodies. In a very broad sense, an observatory may be defined as a place used for looking at natural phenomena. The main types of observatories are astronomical, meteorological, magnetic, and seismological.

The astronomical observatory is the most common and numerous of all observatories. This type of observatory is usually located away from large cities and on high points. The reason for this is to get away from the carbon dioxide and smoke that is found in the atmosphere over cities. It is also necessary that the observatory be free from vibrations that might come from such things as trains and other forms of heavy traffic.

This type of observatory is typically dome-shaped. The upper part of the building, the dome, is free to turn 360 degrees. There is a vertical, slotlike opening in the dome that allows the telescope to be focused, at any point, from the horizon to the zenith.        H. S. G.
SEE ALSO: ASTRONOMY, RADIO TELESCOPE, SPECTROSCOPE, TELESCOPE

**Occipital lobe** see Brain

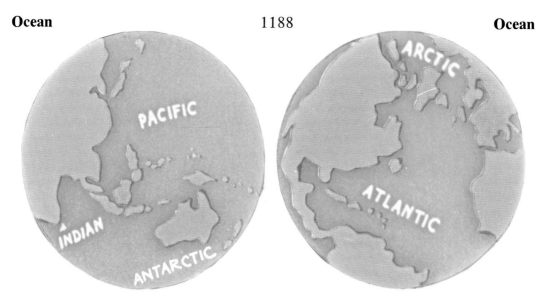

**Oceanographers consider all the large bodies of water on Earth part of the five main oceans.**

**Ocean** Three-fourths of the earth's surface is covered by water. Most of this vast area makes up the four oceans of the world, all of which are interconnected. Other bodies of water called seas and gulfs are really parts of the Pacific, Atlantic, Indian, and Arctic oceans. More than 95 percent of all the water on earth is contained in these four great oceans.

Oceans supply most of the moisture that eventually falls on land as rain. Rivers and streams carry much of the water back to the oceans. Oceans also help to control temperatures around the world and provide the home for a wide variety of plants and animals. Scientists who study oceans are called *oceanographers.*

### ORIGIN

Many theories about the origin of the ocean have been proposed. These theories deal with two important questions: How did the ocean basins form; and where did the water needed to fill these basins come from? The first deals with the varying densities of rock in the earth's crust and the theory of CONTINENTAL DRIFT. The second concerns the composition of the earth's interior and a process called *degassing.*

The first of these theories is based on the fact that the rock underlying the ocean floors is heavier than the rock underlying the continental landmasses. According to this theory, both of these rock masses are "floating" on the semifluid *mantle* which lies far below the surface of the earth. The heavier rock below the ocean floor sinks farther into the mantle, leaving large depressions that are filled with water. These depressions form the world's oceans.

The second theory states that the composition of the earth's interior contains large amounts of water in the form of steam. During volcanic eruptions large amounts of steam are released to the atmosphere and later condense to form rain. It is believed that widespread volcanic activity was very common in the early history of the earth. From this early period of intense volcanic activity and from continual eruptions since, the ocean basins have gradually filled.

### DIVISIONS

The four main oceans of the world are the Pacific, Atlantic, Indian, and Arctic oceans. Some people refer to a fifth ocean, called the Antarctic (or Southern) Ocean, which surrounds the continent of ANTARCTICA. Oceanographers increasingly view the Antarctic Ocean as really a part of Pacific, Atlantic, and Indian oceans.

Since all are connected in one way or another, the oceans of the world are really just one vast body of water. As a result, they have an interchange of water from one ocean to another.

## FEATURES OF THE OCEAN

The ocean is highly complex. Research of its surface includes study of waves, tides, currents, and wind patterns. Below the surface other important features demand careful study; salt content, temperature, deep currents, light penetration, sedimentation, and topography.

Ocean water contains about 35 parts salt to 1000 parts water. It is important to determine variations of this proportion. Another study measures temperatures in the ocean, which vary from about 28° F. (-2.2° C.) in the polar regions to about 96° F. (35.6° C.) in the Persian Gulf.

Light is an important governing factor in the distribution of life. As light penetrates sea water, its yellow, orange, and red rays fade first. After that the green and blue rays fade out at about 1000 feet (305 meters). In very clear water, violet rays may penetrate somewhat deeper, but below this is the watery world of perpetual darkness.

## SEASONS

An alternation of seasons similar to that on land takes place in the seas. In winter waters are dark and cold. Winter gales churn the surface water and cold water is constantly settling toward the deep. In spring the days grow longer, the surface warms, and the wind abates.

## IMPORTANCE

Because water is a "storehouse" for heat, the ocean acts in many ways to regulate the earth's weather. Rainfall, snow, temperature, wind, and storms are closely related to the ocean and the great AIR MASSES which move over it.

The ocean is also important commercially because of its vast resources. Fish, seals and whales, seaweed, and algae are important as sources of food, iodine, and fertilizer. In recent years oil has been discovered under the ocean floor along the continental shelves. Salt and important minerals are to be found in enormous quantities in the sea. More silver than has ever been mined is dissolved in the water of the sea, and there is enough gold dissolved in the ocean to make every person on earth wealthy. However, most of these minerals cannot as yet be recovered economically, and man must wait for improved methods before much of the mineral wealth of the sea can be used. The sea also yields pearls, long prized by people.

Tiny living things in the ocean may give the water color

There are trenches in the ocean that are deeper than the highest mountains are high

Animals may feed on primitive plants, such as seaweeds without roots, leaves, or stems

Warm, tropical ocean waters may hold brightly-colored fish

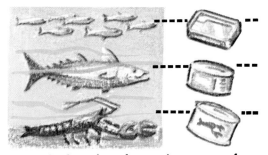

Many food products for man's use come from the ocean.

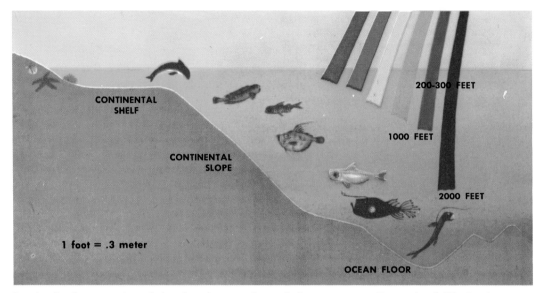

The depth of penetration of the six primary colors of the spectrum affect animal life in the ocean

### THE FUTURE OF OCEANS

Oceanographers have long hoped that the world's oceans might provide new sources of food, energy, desalinated water, and minerals for the world's growing human population. Recently, however, POLLUTION and overuse have threatened to reduce, rather than increase, these opportunities. Coastal waters around many populated areas now show serious signs of pollution. Fish and other forms of sea life are being harvested faster than they can be renewed naturally.

Pollution may present the greatest threat to the health of the world's oceans. In recent years, vast amounts of PETROLEUM, through tanker accidents and offshore drilling leaks, have been released in ocean waters. Oceans have been used as dumping grounds for many solid and liquid wastes, including dangerous nuclear materials. Coastal wetlands, an important breeding area for ocean life, have also been drastically altered. By 1992, for example, 91 percent of California's salt marshes and other Pacific shore wetlands had been drained or otherwise eliminated.    R.N.J./J.H.
SEE ALSO: BALANCE OF NATURE; BIOLOGY; CURRENTS, OCEAN; GRAND BANKS; MARINE BIOLOGY; OCEANOGRAPHY; PELAGIC; PLANKTON; SARGASSUM; SEA WATER; WEATHER

**Ocean currents** see Currents, ocean; International Geophysical Year: Ocean; Oceanography

**Ocean life** see Marine biology

**Oceanography** (oh-shuh-NAHG-ruhf-ee) Oceanography is the name given to the study of the ocean, its basin, and its living creatures. Since ancient times men have been interested in the sea. They have wanted to know about waves, tides, currents, winds, temperature, and the water.

Ocean water contains all the natural ELEMENTS. The sea also contains millions of living creatures. Many of them are important food sources for people. The great valleys and mountains on the bottom of the ocean, and the beaches also, present clues to the story of how the earth was formed and how it is changing.

In order to study the topography and sediment, the dynamics of the water, and the life within the water, the oceanographer has had to invent many new instruments and methods.

### ORIGIN

The modern science of oceanography began about a hundred years ago with the work of three men. In 1841, Matthew Maury, an American naval officer, was placed in charge of the depot of charts and

Mart Toggweiler; U. S. Navy photo

**Ocean research may be done in different ways. Bathyscaphe _Trieste_ (right) descended deep into the ocean and men could observe in safety. Individuals can also descend for experimentation (left), such as for releasing dye to study direction of ocean currents**

instruments. His book, *The Physical Geography of the Sea,* based on his systematic study of currents, tides, and channels, marks the beginning of physical oceanography.

Edward Forbes, born on the Isle of Man, made extensive studies of sea-life from 1836-1842. From his research on both shallow and deep sea iife, the modern science of marine biology began.

A third man, Charles Wyville Thompson, is important as the leader of a famous expedition of the British research ship *Challenger.* In 1872, the vessel began a three-and-one-half year voyage which covered every ocean, and resulted in a collection of thousands of specimens and measurements.

In spite of these first systematic efforts, progress was slow. Since World War II, however, the number of professional oceanographers has increased; and the literature dealing with their work has grown by leaps and bounds.

### SUBJECTS OF STUDY

The material which is studied by oceanographers can be roughly divided into two large classes: the ocean itself, and the ocean basin which also includes beaches.

a. *The ocean:* In addition to the measurements of tides, waves, currents, and temperatures, water samples are continually being analyzed. All the natural ELEMENTS are present in some form in sea water, at least in trace amounts. Various SALT compounds, however, are found in abundance. The most common is sodium chloride, ordinary table

salt. In recent years, the amount of pollution in ocean waters, especially along coastlines, has been increasing. A growing concern among oceanographers is the measurement of this changing chemistry and its effect on ocean life.

Closely related to the chemical composition of sea water is the marine life that inhabits it. Marine biologists gather specimens of living creatures for study. New devices enabling the biologist to remain under water for long periods of time have made it possible to study many of these creatures in their natural surroundings.

b. *The basin:* It was believed earlier that the ocean basin was a huge, scooped-out hole which was very nearly smooth. Now it is known that the ocean floor is much like the land mass of the earth in its irregularity. It is marked off into great mountain ranges, volcanoes, sea mounts, deep canyons, and trenches, as well as level plains. Most of the islands of the sea are in reality the exposed tops of high mountains arising from the ocean floor.

At the base of some larger islands, the submarine earth crust has shifted, leaving gigantic gashes called "trenches." Some are so deep that Mount Everest could be dropped into them, leaving hundreds of feet of water covering it.

There are more trenches in the Pacific than elsewhere. Deepest is the Mariana Trench with its Challenger Deep 36,600 feet (11,156 meters) to the bottom. Other important Pacific trenches are the Mindanao

1191

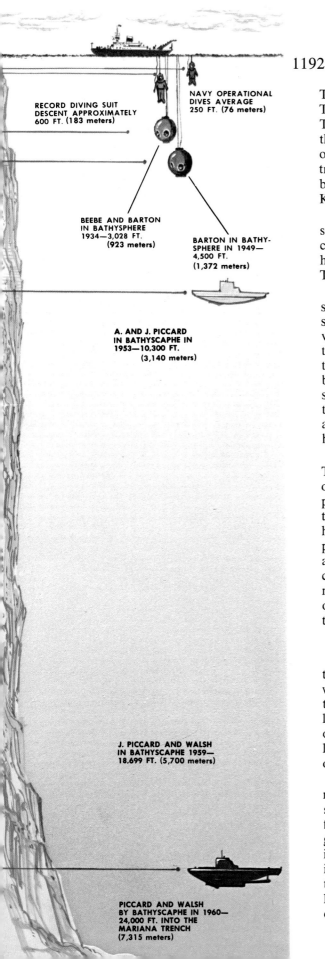

RECORD DIVING SUIT
DESCENT APPROXIMATELY
600 FT. (183 meters)

NAVY OPERATIONAL
DIVES AVERAGE
250 FT. (76 meters)

BEEBE AND BARTON
IN BATHYSPHERE
1934—3,028 FT.
(923 meters)

BARTON IN BATHY-
SPHERE IN 1949—
4,500 FT.
(1,372 meters)

A. AND J. PICCARD
IN BATHYSCAPHE IN
1953—10,300 FT.
(3,140 meters)

J. PICCARD AND WALSH
IN BATHYSCAPHE 1959—
18.699 FT. (5,700 meters)

PICCARD AND WALSH
BY BATHYSCAPHE IN 1960—
24,000 FT. INTO THE
MARIANA TRENCH
(7,315 meters)

Trench southeast of the Philippines, and the Tonga Trench and its companion Kermadec Trench, both near the islands for which they are named. Arching across the floor of the north Pacific are three more large trenches named for the islands at whose bases they lie. They are the Japan, the Kurile, and the Aleutian trenches.

The bottom topography of the Atlantic seems to be mostly ridges and mountain chains. There are several important trenches, however; the best-known is the Romanche Trench, east of Brazil in the mid-Atlantic.

The continental shelves are often deeply scored by great canyons; some of them are several thousand feet (or meters) deep with very steep walls. No satisfactory explanations has yet been offered for their existence. Some seem to have been scoured out by large rivers emptying into the sea thousands of years ago when sea level was lower than at present. This does not explain them all, however, since many are too deep to have been formed in this way.

Sedimentary deposits are carefully studied. These deposits may be composed of shells of tiny animals, or sand, mud, clay, and dust particles. By their thicknesses and the nature of material included in them, sediments help establish the age of the sea. The composition often poses a problem since many areas of the ocean floor are constantly swept clean by deep-water currents. Other sediments are built up by the downward sliding of thick layers of material dislodged by turbidity currents.

### METHODS OF STUDY

a. *Problems:* Man has adapted to life in the air. The lack of air, tremendous underwater pressure, cold, and darkness combine to keep him from penetrating, for any length of time, the deep ocean to observe it directly. With suitable apparatus these problems have been somewhat, but imperfectly, overcome.

Another serious problem is presented by measuring apparatus. Depth cameras, for instance, can photograph portions of the floor of the ocean. But even a good photograph represents only a tiny bit of random information, hardly enough to reveal a clear impression of the ocean. It is something like trying to decide what one's home town looks like by photographing worm holes in someone's back yard.

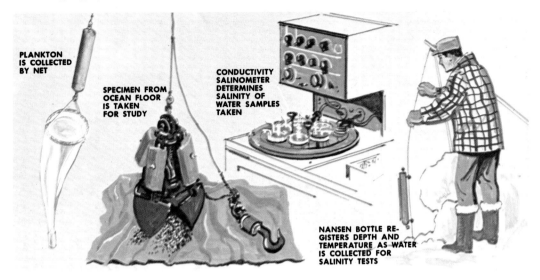

PLANKTON IS COLLECTED BY NET

SPECIMEN FROM OCEAN FLOOR IS TAKEN FOR STUDY

CONDUCTIVITY SALINOMETER DETERMINES SALINITY OF WATER SAMPLES TAKEN

NANSEN BOTTLE RE-GISTERS DEPTH AND TEMPERATURE AS WATER IS COLLECTED FOR SALINITY TESTS

Also, nearly all measuring equipment is suspended from a ship. This means that it is difficult to control the equipment itself. Wires may snap, equipment may break on unseen rocks, and currents may deflect the wires, making the readings inaccurate. Furthermore, it is seldom possible to locate the position of a ship more accurately than within a few miles, although improved navigation instruments and radio have helped correct errors of calculation.

One way to overcome these problems is to simulate in the laboratory the conditions to be studied. Efforts have been made and some success achieved, mostly in studying waves and currents.

b. *Interrelated sciences:* Oceanography is a composite of many sciences. Cooperation among many researchers is required, therefore, to unfold the story of the sea.

The chemist is concerned mainly with the composition of the materials which make up the sea and the basin, and the contents of both. He wants to know the origin and composition of each substance, and the relation of the substance to other materials and to the creatures living in the water.

The geophysicist is mainly interested in the movements and changes in the water. He studies the tides, the formation and action of waves, tidal waves, currents, heat loss and absorption, ice formation, and pressure.

Marine biologists are interested in the answers to such questions as: What types of creatures inhabit the ocean? Where do they come from? Why did they develop the way they did? Why do they live in one place and not in another? How are they related?

What part do they play in the economy of the ocean?

The geologist studies undersea volcanos, rock formations, trenches, earth fractures, and sediments. He observes the shifting beaches, and probes the continental shelves and slopes, attempting to determine how the continents were formed, if the islands are being lifted up or sinking, and how the gigantic mountain chains were buried under immeasurable tons of salt water.

Finally, meteorologists are engaged in studying the important role the ocean plays in making weather. They are working hard to find the relations among earth, air, sun, and water, and how these factors create calm, wind, storms, snow, and rain.

c. *Instruments:* The oceanographer must have special instruments for his work. These instruments may be roughly divided into three types: those for collecting specimens; those for making measurements; and those which make diving possible.

*Sampling apparatus:* In this first group the most common apparatus includes plankton nets, water bottles, bottom corers, and dredges. Nets have been designed to be suspended below, and towed behind, ships. Because it is important to know from what depths the samples come, these nets can be tightly closed like an umbrella while being lowered to the desired depth. At any depth, a weight can be dropped down the cable suspending the net to trip the mechanism holding the net closed. The net balloons out, and, as it is towed, traps whatever enters it. A second weight is dropped to trip the mechanism to close the net.

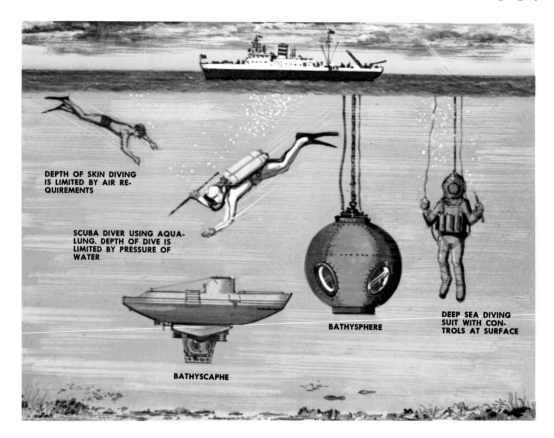

DEPTH OF SKIN DIVING IS LIMITED BY AIR REQUIREMENTS

SCUBA DIVER USING AQUALUNG. DEPTH OF DIVE IS LIMITED BY PRESSURE OF WATER

BATHYSPHERE

DEEP SEA DIVING SUIT WITH CONTROLS AT SURFACE

BATHYSCAPHE

**The depths to which man can descend into the ocean have been limited to the capacity of his apparatus to withstand pressures**

Water bottles are designed, usually with only minor variations, after the famous Nansen bottle, named for the Scandinavian oceanographer who invented it. The bottle is open at both ends. When attached to a wire and submerged, water flows freely through the bottle until it has reached the desired depth. A weight is dropped down the wire to trip a mechanism which closes both ends of the bottle, trapping the water in it. Several bottles can be used at one time at various depths. Each bottle, as it closes, releases a second weight which drops to the bottle below, repeating the process.

Thermometers are built into the bottles. The bottle can be turned upside down to fix the column of mercury in the thermometer. In this way the temperature of the sea at any depth can be measured.

Early coring tubes were long, hollow tubes, one end of which was sharpened, the other heavily weighted to drive the tube into the sediment. In 1935 Dr. C. S. Piggot improved this instrument by including an explosive charge at the weighted end; when the charge was set off at the proper time, the tube could be driven to a depth of about 10 feet (3 meters). Kullenberg devised a piston corer some years later that made use of the enormous water pressure at the bottom to suck the core up into the tube and at the same time drive the tube deeper. Cores 70 feet (21.3 meters) long can be obtained with this tube.

*Measuring instruments:* This group is represented by the weight and line which is still occasionally used to measure depth. This procedure is called *sounding*.

The first major improvement came with the invention of sonic sounders which employed the principle of sound reflection. A hammer struck the metal hull of the ship to send sound waves out from the ship. By measuring the length of time it took for an echo to return from the ocean bottom, the depth of the water could be determined. Supersonic devices have since been perfected which automatically record the depth on a moving paper tape, and at the same time eliminate the nuisance of the noise.

## Ocelot

A variation of sonic sounding is seismic sounding. A small explosive charge of nitroglycerine, or other explosive, is set off under the surface of the ocean, and echoes returning from the bottom indicate both the apparent bottom of the ocean and also the depth of the sediment by echoing from the rock bottom underneath it.

*Diving apparatus:* The practice of diving dates back to the earliest civilizations, but only in the last century has really satisfactory equipment for use at great depths under water been developed. This does not mean that suits, bells, and the like had not been thought of much earlier, but that they were generally unsuccessful.

The diving apparatus must perform two basic functions. It must supply air for the diver under water, and it must protect him from great pressure while allowing him to move about. No diving apparatus has yet overcome all of these difficulties.

The traditional suit is an effective device, enabling considerable depth and freedom of movement; but it depends on a surface source of air, thus limiting depth.

Two other types of diving apparatus have been developed. The first is the aqualung, or Self Contained Underwater Breathing Apparatus (SCUBA). The device permits almost unlimited freedom of movement, but limits the depth of the dive to somewhat over 200 feet (61 meters). The other is the bathysphere, a heavy steel ball that can be lowered to great depth, but practically no freedom of movement is provided in it.

Within the past few decades, the bathyscaphe has been developed. The bathyscaphe has, to some extent, solved both problems. It has achieved the deepest known depth of the ocean—nearly 7 miles (11.3 kilometers) down. Its small electric motor allows it to move over a limited area of ocean floor.

Computerized sensors and recording instruments, often linked by satellite communications, have simplified some aspects of oceanography recently. Unmanned buoys, for example, can transmit measurements to land-based research centers. R.N.J.

SEE ALSO: CURRENTS, OCEAN; DEPTH SOUNDING GLOMAR CHALLENGER; OCEAN; PELAGIC PLANKTON; PLATE TECTONICS; SEA LEVEL; SEA WATER; TIDES; WAVES

**Ocelot** see Cat family

J. W. Thompson
**An octopus of the China coast**

**Ochoa, Servero** (1905- ) Ochoa, a Spanish-American biochemist, shared in the 1959 NOBEL PRIZE in physiology and medicine. His work dealt with the syntheses of ribonucleic acid (RNA) and protein.

In 1955, Ochoa isolated from a form of bacteria *(Aztobacter vinelandii)* an enzyme that proved capable of initiating the formation of RNA from nucleotides. Arthur Kornberg, a former student of Ochoa's and co-winner of the 1959 NOBEL PRIZE, succeeded in a similar experiment that led to the synthesis of DNA. Also, Ochoa achieved the test-tube syntheses of proteins. This led to a better understanding of how proteins form in humans and other animals. P.P.S.

**Octopus** (AHK-tuh-puhs) An octopus is a mollusk related to clams and oysters. It lives in many parts of the world, in both deep and shallow water. It is sometimes known as the *devilfish,* but it is not a fish. It has a round body, large head, and large eyes. An octopus has eight arms. In size, octopi range from 2 inches (5 centimeters) to 28 feet (8.5 meters) from arm tip to arm tip. They vary in color and are able to change color.

Most octopi move around for food at night. Crabs are their favorite food although they eat other crustaceans and fish. Their strong beaked jaws are used for crushing shells of crustaceans.

The octopus is able to swim rapidly, moving backwards and trailing its arms. It propels itself by ejecting water through a siphon-like structure. It can also walk rapidly along the ocean floor. For protection, it ejects an ink-like substance, coloring the surrounding water.

The internal structure of the octopus is similar to that of a SQUID. The third right arm of the male is enlarged and modified as a copulatory organ. The female deposits eggs, either in rope-like strings or grape-like clusters, on the roof of its hiding place. It guards the eggs which hatch in six to eight weeks. Along the Pacific Coast, from Alaska to Lower California, *Octopus bimaculatus* may be found. This kind is less numerous today than formerly. It is generally gray with two large red spots on the back. *Octopus bairdi* is found along the Atlantic Coast. This kind is bluish-white, speckled with brown. It has an arm span of 40 inches (102 centimeters). I. H. S.

SEE ALSO: MOLLUSCA

**Oersted, Hans Christian** (ER-stedd) (1777-1851) Hans Christian Oersted was the Danish physicist and chemist who founded the branch of science called *electromagnetism*. Electromagnetism deals with magnetic fields developed by ELECTRICITY.

During an evening lecture at the University of Copenhagen where Oersted served as professor, he accidentally discovered that a magnetic needle was deflected by an electrical current. This discovery established him as one of the outstanding physicists of his age. After experimenting, Oersted discovered that every conductor which carries an electrical current is surrounded by a magnetic field. This experiment, now known as the "Oersted Experiment," proved that electricity can produce magnetism. In 1934 the "Oersted" was adopted as the unit of measurement of the strength of a magnetic field. D. H. J.

SEE ALSO: ELECTROMAGNET, PHYSICS

**Offset** see Printing

**Ohm** The ohm is the unit of resistance to the passage of an electric current. The ohm is the resistance causing a potential drop of one absolute VOLT when a steady current of one absolute AMPERE flows through it.

SEE: ELECTRICITY, MEASUREMENT, OHMMETER

**Georg Ohm**

**Ohm, Georg Simon** (1787-1854) Georg Simon Ohm was a German physicist who is best known for Ohm's Law of electric conduction. This law states that the current, $I$, that flows in a circuit multiplied by the amount of resistance, $R$, is equal to the applied voltage, $E$. The law may be stated in symbols as $E = I \times R$. The OHM, the unit of electrical resistance, is named in his honor. He is also known for work in mathematics and acoustics.

Ohm was born in Erlanger, Germany, on March 16, 1787. After attending the local university, he was, in 1817, appointed professor of mathematics at the Jesuits' College at Cologne. He remained there until 1833 when he resigned to join the faculty of the Polytechnic School of Nuremberg. In 1849, he accepted an appointment as professor of mathematics at Munich. Ohm's numerous writings were of somewhat inferior quality. One exception was a pamphlet published in Berlin in 1827 which contained a summary of what is now known as Ohm's Law. His work was coldly received by his fellow scientists, and Georg Ohm was so deeply hurt that he resigned his position at the Jesuits' College, Cologne. His work began to be recognized, however, and in 1841 he was awarded the Copley Medal of the Royal Society in London. One year later he was made a foreign member of the Society. D. H. J.

SEE ALSO: ELECTRICITY, OHMMETER

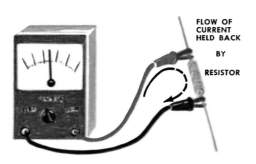

FLOW OF
CURRENT
HELD BACK

BY

RESISTOR

If all the current flowed through the resistor, the number of ohms would be zero. A decrease in current through the meter corresponds to the increased resistance offered by the unknown resistor. The ohmmeter scale reads more as less current flows

**Ohmmeter** (OHM-mee-ter) An ohmmeter is an instrument for showing how many ohms of resistance there are to the passage of an electric current.

Since the exact measurement of resistance is slow, various types of ohmmeters have been invented to give direct readings in ohms.

The ohm is that resistance which causes a potential drop of one absolute VOLT when a steady current of one absolute AMPERE flows through it. The international ohm is based on a specified conductor. It is the resistance of a uniform thread of mercury in a capillary tube of such diameter that the thread is 106.3 cm. long, weighs 14.4521 grams, and has a temperature of 0 degrees Centigrade.               V. V. N.

SEE ALSO: ELECTRICITY

**Oil** An oil is a fluid light enough to float on water. It will not mix with water but will combine with alcohol. It remains fluid at normal temperatures. This distinguishes the oils from *fats,* which are solid at normal temperatures.

A few oils come from fishes and other animals, such as fish oils and fish-liver oils, whale oil and neat's-foot oil. The latter is processed from the feet of animals at meat-packing plants. Sperm oil from the whale is not a true oil but a liquid wax.

Most of our useful oils are obtained from the ground, as are petroleum and other mineral products, or from plants.

The ancient Chinese, Hindus, Egyptians, Greeks and Romans obtained vegetable oils by milling and pressing various plant parts. Today most vegetable oils are obtained by heating or steaming methods.

Many different kinds of plant life provide useful oils: almond oil (from the nuts), castor oil (from the seeds of the castor bean), coconut oil (from kernels of nuts), corn oil (from the kernels), cottonseed oil, olive oil (from the fruit), peanut oil (from the peanuts), and soybean oil (from the beans). Petroleum and the products made from it are used as fuels and in chemicals.

Some of the important uses for oils of various kinds are in lubrication, flavoring, perfume, and medicines.               J. A. C.

SEE ALSO: FAT, OIL GLAND, PETROLEUM

**Oil gland** Almost all oil glands open into a hair root (follicle). A few, like oil glands on the eyelids, discharge their oil directly on the skin surface. The soles of the feet and the palms of the hands lack oil glands.

These glands are saclike or *alveolar* glands. Several alveolar secretory *pieces* empty into a common duct which empties into the hair follicle. Around the secretory endpieces is a CONNECTIVE TISSUE capsule.

The cells in the endpieces secrete fat. Fat drops form in the CYTOPLASMS of these cells. Small drops, when they touch, run together to make bigger drops. Nuclei shrink and cells break down into a mass of fat and cellular debris. Cells become distended and the plasma membranes around them break. The mixture of oil and cellular debris (*sebum*) is discharged. This type of secretion, in which the secretory cell is destroyed by the process of secretion, is called *holocrine secretion.* Destroyed cells are replaced by basal cells in the glandular endpieces.               J. C. K.

SEE ALSO: SKIN MODIFICATIONS

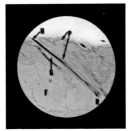

An oil gland in the scalp is seen at G. H is the hair; P, the pigment; R, the hair follicle; F, the fat cells

Photo-micrograph by National Teaching Aids, Inc.

# Conversion Factors to Metric Measurement

### Length
1 inch = 25.4 millimeters (mm) exactly
1 inch = 2.54 centimeters (cm) exactly
1 foot = 0.3048 meters (m) exactly
1 yard = 0.9144 meters (m) exactly
1 mile = 1.609344 kilometers (km) exactly

### Area
1 square inch = 6.4516 square centimeters ($cm^2$) exactly
1 square foot = 0.092903 square meters ($m^2$)
1 square yard = 0.836127 square meters ($m^2$)
1 square acre = 0.404686 hectares (ha)
1 square mile = 2.58999 square kilometers ($km^2$)

### Cubic Measure
1 cubic inch = 16.387064 cubic centimeters ($cm^3$) exactly
1 cubic foot = 0.0283168 cubic meters ($m^3$)
1 cubic yard = 0.764555 cubic meters ($m^3$)

### US Liquid Measure
1 fluid ounce = 29.5735 milliliters (ml)
1 fluid ounce = 0.2957 deciliters (dl)
1 pint = 0.473176 liters (l)
1 gallon = 3.78541 liters (l)

### US Dry Measure
1 pint = 0.550610 liters (l)
1 bushel = 35.2391 liters (l)

### Weight
1 grain = 0.0647989 grams (g)
1 ounce = 28.3495 grams (g)
1 pound = 0.453592 kilograms (kg)
1 short ton = 0.907185 metric tons (t)
1 UK ton = 1.01605 metric tons (t)

### Temperature
To convert Fahrenheit to Centigrade (Celsius) complete the following equation. $(F° - 32) \times 5 \div 9 = C°$